FOREWORD

This Book originally took shape with the collaboration of Richard F. Allen, whose contribution to the solution of presentational difficulties is beyond the measure of mere words to express.

Then, again, the encouragement given to the author by Dr. B. V. Raman, the eminent and versatile Editor of The Astrological Magazine and Shri H. G. Mirchandani, an enlightened publisher of books himself, is the source of perseverence of this author, which brought his MSS. to bed at JAICO'S printing. It is now for the readers to say whether all these efforts by eminent persons who have other worthwhile activities and this unknown author have been, indeed, necessary or not.

In fine, the Book is dedicated to PADMANABHA SUBRAMANIAM, founder and President of The Sringeri Sri Sarada Peedam Sankara Hall in Calcutta, a magnificent institution devoted to the propagation of Vedanta in all its aspects.

Y. Keshava Menon

FOREWORD

This Book originally took shape with the collaboration of Richard H. Allen, whose contribution to the solution of presentational difficulties is beyond the measure of mere words to express.

Then again, the encouragement given to the author by Dr. B. V. Raman, the eminent and versatile Editor of The Astrological Magazine and Shri H. G. Mirchandani, an enlightened publisher of books himself, is the source of perseverance of this author, which brought his MSS. to bed at LATTO'S printing. It is now for the readers to say whether all these efforts by eminent persons who have other worthwhile activities and this unknown author have been, indeed, necessary or not.

In fine, the Book is dedicated to PADMANABHA SUBRAMANIAM, (founder and President of The Sringeri Sarada Peedam Sankara Hall in Calcutta), a magnificent institution devoted to the propagation of Vedanta in all its aspects.

V. Kesava Menon

THE MIND OF ADI SHANKARA

by

Y. Keshava Menon

JAICO PUBLISHING HOUSE
Bombay ● Delhi ● Bangalore ● Calcutta
Hyderabad ● Madras

The Mind of Adi Shankara

ISBN: 81-7224-214-X

First Jaico Impression: 1976
Second Jaico Impression: 1980
Third Jaico Impression: 1989
Fourth Jaico Impression: 1993

Published by
Ashwin J. Shah
Jaico Publishing House
121, M.G. Road
Bombay-400 023.

Printed by
R. N. Kothari
Konam Printers
Universal Factory Compound
Diana Talkies Lane
Tardeo
Bombay 400 034.

CONTENTS

CONTENTS

INTRODUCTION

Though he is considered one of the foremost of India's philosophers, Shankara is also one of the most misunderstood. We have heard fire-eating revolutionaries advance the theory that the essence of Shankara's philosophy is on all fours with the materialistic interpretation of life formulated by Hegel, on which is built the edifice of Marxism. Pandit Jawaharlal Nehru, in the course of his record of the cultural history of the world, testifies to Shankara's merits as an outstanding Shaivite. In his own time, Shankara was hailed as Shanmathasthapanacharya (founder of six faiths). Obviously all of them cannot very well be right.

Much of the misunderstanding of Shankara's position may be due to the absence of a lucid presentation of his life and works in a comprehensive and readable form. This short monograph is an attempt to meet that need for the benefit of those who have no previous acquaintance with philosophy.

Doing this is in the nature of giving a popular image to a classical theme. It has meant taking upon ourselves the daunting task of trying to hold the attention of readers whose minds are neither tilled nor rendered fertile to receive the seeds of the subject. We have thereby presented ourselves with a formidable problem of presentation. In particular there is the problem of terminology.

Traditionally, Indian philosophy has been expressed in what must be the most subtle, extensive and precise terminology for abstract ideas ever invented. The preoccupation of its ancient founding fathers with language itself was almost incredible. Even to warrant being taken notice of, any discourse on philosophy had to be word-perfect. Grammar was given the status of Veda-Vedanta, the Veda of the ends of the Vedas. It was not unusual for an aspirant to the study of philosophy to be ground through the discipline and rigorous study of grammar for as much as a decade and a half before the first word in philosophic parlance was whispered in his ears. No contemporary student of philosophy would consider such a process of learning worth his while; he would feel that life is too short to study philology and philosophy at the same time. The leisure that informed the schools of the ancients is conspicuous by its absence in the world of today.

It is cold comfort to the reader to be told that the classical terms employed by Shankara correspond to real entities unless he is provided with equivalents that he can understand. At the same time, the question of terminology cannot be completely avoided in this way. All philosophies have their specialised terminologies and need them to make themselves understandable; indeed it is often true to say that when the student has grasped the meaning of the terms he has grasped the philosophy itself. We have tried to avoid jargon and have sought for English equivalents for the principal Sanskrit concepts, but this objective can never be fully achieved. The dilemma remains. If on the one hand the Sanskrit terms are used freely, the result would be so rebarbative that the non-specialist student might be forgiven for abandoning the whole thing. "Saguna Brahman is Nirguna Brahman conceived empirically; the former is vyavaharika while the latter is paramarthika" is a near-exact statement, but the ordinary citizen of a secular society cannot be expected to read 200 pages of that sort of language.

On the other hand the nearest English approximations to the Sanskrit terms—"idealism", "illusion", "sin", "personal God"—often import into the discourse, in addition to downright inaccuracy, the implications of European philosophy and of Christianity, and thus lead to confusion rather than clarity.

We have compromised by introducing the basic Sanskrit terms essential to the presentation, but have simultaneously tried to outline the superstructure without very extensive terminology.

But even if all the purely presentational problems could be solved, the fundamental difficulty would remain—the Indian pre-supposition that intellectual knowledge is not, as many Europeans tacitly believe, the only means or the

only end. To the Hindu, learning is only a part of life—
at best a gateway to a higher or better way of life based
on an intuitive perception of truth which cannot be caught
in words, however eloquent. It cannot be caught in words
because truth must, axiomatically, be perfect, but words
are not perfect, because the phenomenon of life itself is
not perfect. Any efforts at lucidity are, therefore, in some
degree foredoomed to failure, regardless of the writers'
skill. At best, the result may seem a strange mixture of
the painfully obvious and the impossibly difficult. It is
only a partial answer to say that life itself is like that;
but if the book appeals to those who regard philosophy
as something more than a "subject" or "interest" or
"hobby", its method may not have been a complete failure.

What distinguishes the Indian philosopher from the
large community of Western philosophers is that the
purely analytical, intellectual or logical approach is in-
sufficient to the Indian. He holds firmly to the view that
a philosophy properly so-called, as Marcus Aurelius would
have used the term, is a means to leading a better life or
it is nothing. And "better" to an Indian has an axiomatic meaning which is common to practically all variants
of his philosophy. For instance, his search for the ultimate truth is not jumping across a ditch from the bank
of falsehood to the bank of truth; it is a laborious climb
on the ladder bearing rungs of various levels of relative
truth. Nothing is, indeed, absolutely or finally false. The
psychological technique employed in this search for the
ultimate reality is a species of meditation which has an
interesting resemblance to the technique of Western psy-
choanalysis. "Good actions" and even a personal God are
often valued only as an adjunct to this technique, as pegs,
so to say, on which to hang the modes of the mind.

This may seem to the contemporary student immured
in the West-oriented education an empirical and topsy-
turvy approach to philosophy, but if he reflects more
deeply he will come to see that it is at least not an irrational or superstitious approach. There is nothing in Indian
philosophy that is inconsistent with the scientific approach
to life. It frankly recognizes the existence of more than

one level of thought and sees no difficulty in regarding a man as simultaneously a body obeying physical and biological laws, a complex of mental and sensory processes capable of feeling love and producing music, and a soul identical in nature with the Creator Himself. Thus the Indian avoids the "nothing but" philosophies, and in particular the dilemma of the scientific materialist who regards ideas as "only" a by-product of the chemical processes in the brain. The Indian view may or may not be "true", but it is at least rational and does no violence to commonsense.

The attitude of the Indian philosophers towards "revealed religion" is by no means the same as a European's, who invests the term with Christian beliefs, and the reader could easily fall into the mistake of supposing that Shankara "believed" in the Upanishads and related scriptures in the same way as some orthodox Christians believe in the "literal inspiration" of the Bible. Shankara did accept the truth of the traditional scriptures as axiomatic, but he did not regard the letter of them as inspired; if only because he was not tied to "belief in" a personal God portrayed in them. The scriptures were regarded as true because they were true, and the "faith" of Shankara was acquired little by little by sitting at the feet of a master and practising under his guidance the traditional techniques of study and meditation, thus verifying for himself that they achieved the purpose for which they were intended. There are no cataclysmic conversions, but the precise nature of the philosopher's illumination can never be known to others; and even if the student wanted to talk about his experience, he could not do so. This does not mean that there is anything superstitious or magical, or even mysterious, about it. It is simply one of the rules of life as lived by Indian philosophers that "the man who claims he knows, knows nothing; but he who claims nothing, knows".

Another difficulty that often deters today's reader, and tempts him into doing ancient Indian philosophers less than justice and closing his mind against them, is the semi-legendary accounts of their lives which have come down to us claiming biographical status. Most of our knowledge of Shankara is of this semi-legendary kind, but it would be illogical to be put off by such stories. Shankara lived well over a thousand years ago in a country, where—even though it be their own—philosophers were not without honour, and it is inevitable that legends should have been woven around their life and doings. For the Christian, the value of the Gospels would remain if Jesus had never existed. For **him,** the historical existence of Jesus is a certainty. For the **historian,** however, the value of the Gospels would disappear if Jesus was a myth; but that is because the historian is approaching the matter on a different level. Some of the traditional stories of Shankara's life are far from edifying; but his works stand on their own feet, and it would make no difference to a seeker of knowledge if those works were the invention of a Portuguese or a Hottentot. For those who are curious, the salient fables and facts available about Shankara's life are given in the Appendix.

On the intellectual level, Indian philosophy is logical and rational and proceeds on the same kinds of axioms, overt or implied, as Western philosophy. Shankara was one of the most subtle of Indian philosophers, and though for him intellectual dexterity was not an end in itself, the reader will find some reasoning worthy of his steel in the following pages. Equally, however, it would be an error to bring to Shankara the same spirit of mesmerised reverence that many Christians bring to the Elizabethan English of the Authorised Version of the Bible. Reverence and blind faith are also not enough. Perhaps the most helpful thing that can be said is that the reader who wants to get the best out of Shankara should approach him with a cool, open, constructively-critical mind, but determined to study the philosophy as a whole and not to reject conclusions out of hand. There is ratiocination in plenty for him, but if he is not prepared to test the philosophy for himself, he would have gained little from Shankara.

We never intended this little book to be a scholar's delight, but at the same time we have been at pains to ensure that no facet of Shankara's teachings has been misrepresented. The original MS. (which has not been

appreciably changed in substance) was read through by
the late Prof. S. K. Belvalkar and Shri Shri Shankara-
charya of Kurtkoti—two of the most celebrated authori-
ties on the subject—and approved by them.

We admit to having laced our narratives with some
light-hearted banter. There is nothing in the rule-books
of philosophy that insists that philosophy must eschew all
that is not severe and sombre. Shankara himself employed
much wit and humour in driving home certain points
which would otherwise have remained caviar to the
general.

THE MIND OF ADI SHANKARA

The General Background

Before we can consider Shankara's special contribution to Indian philosophy, we must look briefly at the general framework in which his work was accomplished.

The basic scriptures of the Hindus are called the Vedas. They are in Sanskrit, which bears somewhat the same relation to modern Indian languages and culture as Latin and Greek bear to European languages and culture—although the parallel should not be pressed too far. Sanskrit belongs to the Indo-European family of languages, and bears recognizable affinities to Greek and Latin. It is the parent of the main spoken languages of most of India and Ceylon, and with its vast literature of lyrical, dramatic, and other works—as well as philosophy—it continues to influence the spoken languages. Thus the Vedas are by no means as dead, foreign, or artificial to a Hindu as are Latin and Greek scriptures to a European.

The word "Veda" comes from a root meaning "to know", which is probably allied to the root in the Latin —**videre**—"to see" (**c.f.** French **"voir"**, English "vision") The Vedic literature was grouped at some time in the remote past into four main groups—(1) The Rig-veda (mainly hymns), (2) the Sama-veda (mainly tunes and chants), (3) the Yajur-veda (lore of prayer or sacrificial formulas), and (4) the Atharva-veda (lore of the Atharvans). The volume and complexity of the material is enormous.

The Rig-veda consists of hymns addressed to the elementary forces of nature personified as superhuman beings in a manner reminiscent of Greek mythology. The principal figures are Indra, the god of the cloud regions, and Agni (Latin **ignis**) the god of fire, but there are also references to Father Heaven (Dyaus Pitar = Jupiter) and other deities. The book was probably intended originally as a prayer book for the religious services of the priestly community; but those who collected and reduced the Veda into writing including in it a good number of 'secular and popular lyrics as well as some philosophical pronouncements.

It is very difficult to say how old the Vedic hymns are. Indian history is completely lacking in chronology of the kind we are familiar with, and the many traditions associated with the Vedas, while they may well contain some germ of historical truth, cannot be regarded as evidence. From internal evidence it is clear that the hymns were composed at different dates. The most probable date for their collection is about 1000 B.C., but the majority of them were probably in existence as early as 2000-1500 B.C.

The hymns show the Vedic people as a relatively light-skinned Aryan race settled mainly in the plains of the Punjab and leading the life of herdsmen and husbandmen on land they had conquered from the darker-skinned aboriginal inhabitants. The priestly office was already important, but the caste system had not yet developed.

Attached to the main, or "samhita" part of the Rig-veda are two "Brahmanas"—prose works dealing with the rituals for offerings of rice, milk etc., and with the Soma sacrifice performed with the juice of the "moon-plant".

Each Brahmana is supplemented with a "forest-book" or Aranyaka, the object of which is to provide in place of the sacrificial rules a system of symbolic worship and meditation suitable for the man who, following the Hindu ideal of the holy life, having brought up his family, has consigned the care of the household to them and has become a recluse living in the forest. Certain parts of the Aranyakas constitute the Upanishads. In these sections, liturgy and ritualism are left behind and the works scale the heights of spiritual aspiration.

The Upanishads also exist in many different versions. They are not always consistent with one another, and the writers, who probably wrote them long after the samhita and brahmana portions of the Veda had become standard scriptures, are sometimes at pains to try to reconcile them with the earlier work. This in no way detracts from their value, though it adds to their bewildering complexity.

They grew, like the works of the great mystical teachers in all lands, out of the background of their familiar religion and ritual. The spirit which informs them and the philosophy they teach is universal and everlasting, but the method of expression, the symbolism, is in the terms of the every-day religion of the authors. Those who regard philosophy as a means to living a good life will not be deterred by this; for they will be glad enough of any foothold in their ascent of the Hill Difficulty.

But to return to the Vedas. The Sama-veda consists of two parts—the Samhita and the Gana or tune-book. The Brahmana part of the Sama-veda contains a great deal of technical matter for the benefit of the priests. What is important for us is that the Chandogya and Kena Upanishads are attached to the Sama-veda.

The Yajur-veda exists in several different forms. There are three earlier forms in which sacrificial prayers (yajus) and illustrative prose portions (brahmana) are mixed. These are called the Black (obscure) Yajur-veda. The Upanishads attached to this Veda are the Taittiriya, Mahanarayana, Katha, Svetasvatara and Maitrayani. In a later version the texts were reorganised and the prayers or "mantra" grouped by themselves, followed by a brahmana section. This form was called the White (lucid) Yajur-veda and attached to it were the Isa and the Brihadaranyaka, the last being one of the most important Upanishads. It may be added that there were two different versions of the White Yajur-veda which seem to have been developed in different locales.

The Atharva-veda is considered on linguistic groups to be the latest part of the scriptures to be recognised. It is traditionally associated with two mythical priestly families, the Atharvans and the Angiras, and describes all manner of superstitious practices like magical rites appropriate for people in a much lower stage of social and religious advancement than the educated householders displayed in the other Vedas. This Veda has come down in a much less satisfactory state of preservation than the other three. The Mundaka, Prasna and Mandukya Upanishads belong to the Atharva-veda.

The second great work in the Hindu canon is the Bhagavad Gita. This is a section of an enormous epic poem called the Mahabharata, which is eight times the length of the Odyssey and Iliad combined. As usual, it is very difficult to assign any date to this work, but it is not likely to have been earlier than 300 B.C. or later than 200 A.D. In any case, it was probably developed and revised over a long period. The Bhagavad Gita narrates how the god Krishna in the assumed role of a charioteer discourses to Prince Arjuna on the eve of a battle between two sections of his own family in which he is ranged on one side.

The third canonical work is the Brahma Sutras. A sutra is a short sentence or aphorism, shorn of all verbiage and designed to convey the essence of a religious or philosophical idea in the smallest possible space. Sutras were probably intended originally as mnemonics, and possibly to conserve scarce writing materials. The aim of the Brahma Sutras was to act as a commentary on the Vedas and their attendant Upanishads, and reconcile the apparently conflicting teachings into a logical philosophical exposition. The date of the Brahma Sutras may be anywhere between 500 B.C. and 450 A.D.

The word Vedanta also calls for explanation. By derivation the word means the end of the Vedas, and Hindus often use the word to mean simply the Upanishads, which are both physically the end portions of the Vedas and also metaphorically their goal or culmination or end. The word Vedanta is also used, however to mean the general philosophy taught in the three canonical books described above—the Vedas (particularly the Upanishads), the Brahma Sutras, and the Bhagavad Gita. The three books are sometimes distinguished as the spiritual institute, the rational institute and the institute of tradition. The Vedas and the Brahma Sutras formed the "shruti", the scriptures given by the direct inspiration of God. The Gita was of a simpler kind of scripture called "smriti", which nevertheless also opened the door to liberation and was accessible to all. It was usual for all Vedantic teachers to write commentaries on the three institutes and establish that their doctrine was in full conformity with them.

The sage Shankara, whose works are the subject of this book, probably lived about 800 A.D.—hundreds of years after the three canonical books had become fixed scriptures. His great contribution to Indian philosophy and religion was his commentary on all the three institutes. The authorship of this commentary is established beyond all reasonable doubt, but out of over 400 works attributed to Shankara, Professor Belvalkar, a recognized authority, after close scrutiny finds only twenty four to be genuine. The present book is based mainly on Shankara's commentaries on the scriptures, a metrical-cum-prose work called Upadesasahasri, a poetical work called Vivekachudamani and some hymns.

Shankara founded his work on a great heritage, but it must not be thought that there is therefore something impenetrably Eastern or Hindu about his writings. Difficulties there are in plenty, but on one plane they are the difficulties which all but the sharpest intellects find in grasping the abstruse and the subtle, and on another the difficulty which the striving soul finds in transcending its ego and achieving union with God. The first can be overcome with patience, the second only with devotion, and perhaps with the gift that Christians call "grace".

Before we leave this brief survey of the background against which Shankara's philosophy was written, a few words should be said about Buddhism and its relation to the background. Buddhism arose in the sixth century B.C. as an off-shoot of the prevailing Hindu religion of North India. By this time, the polytheistic Vedas with their brahmana additions were the canonical scriptures of the Hindus. The caste system was well developed, with the priestly caste of Brahmins claiming superiority. The Upanishads were already for the most part in existence.

Buddhism rejected the authority of the Vedas and preached a way of life rather than a religion. It has been said to bear the same relation to Hinduism as Protestantism bears to Catholicism, but this analogy should not be pressed too far. Some contrasts between Buddhism and Shankara's philosophical doctrines will appear in their place later on. It is sufficient now to mention that Buddhism was conveyed to Ceylon in the third century B.C., whence it spread to Burma and Siam and parts of China. It is still a popular religion in those countries and in Japan too; it is no longer a popular force in India. In Shankara's day (ca 780-820) Buddhism in India had apparently sunk to a low level and become in many ways a new superstition.

Sources of Knowledge

It is, in the nature of the subject, impossible to set out in a neat little list of points a philosophy which embraces a complete system of thought and way of life. It may help, however, if we try to summarise the main features of Shankara's system at the outset; after which the various problems will be dealt with one by one. It is not enough to do this, because the philosophy must be grasped as a whole, but the best method available to us seems to be to look at the philosophy from the standpoint of each of its main tenets in turn. There will inevitably be a good deal of repetition, but in the end the student may be able to see the philosophy as a whole. If his interest is already aroused, his best plan is to read straight ahead; many of the questions which arise in his mind will be answered later on, and some of the others may be answered at a second reading.

The fundamental principle of Shankara's teaching is that the pure, innermost "Self" is the ultimate reality. This Self (which must not be confused with the "ego") is a spiritual kernel of the same kind as Brahman or Godhead, the ultimate reality. When a man overcomes ignorance, or "avidya" (the word has a very wide connotation which will be explained later), and grasps intuitively that the Universe is merely an external phenomenon, and realises the identity between the Self and Brahman, he becomes a "liberated" soul, waiting only for his final liberation from the body by death. The Self or Brahman cannot be described, because it has no "qualities" in the ordinary sense, though it is sometimes said to be of the nature of pure being pure consciousness and pure bliss.

The material universe of forms and things is grounded in Brahman, but its formation therefrom cannot be described or formulated. It functions on the basis of the law of "karma", that is, of cause and effect; but its ultimate cause is Brahman, which has created the material world and started the process of change that we see occurring in that world. All creation is, however, "Maya" or the power of illusion. Within the realm of maya the universe exists and can be conceived as a creation of Brahman, who can also be conceived as a personal God; though from the standpoint of ultimate reality even a personal deity is a product of maya. The causal law itself is ultimately unintelligible, because it is an illusory concept of name and form. There is no more essential difference between effect and cause than between a moulded pot and the clay from which it is made. The world as caused by Brahman is an illusory superimposition (adhyasa) of phenomenon on the basic reality—like a rope which is mistaken for a snake or the mirage-lake seen on the desert sand.

It follows logically therefore that Shankara should urge the renunciation of transitory things and the acquisition of "right knowledge" as the only means of attaining "liberation".

The student's first reaction to this bald summary may well be that it is very hard to grasp, and that in so far as it can be grasped it is "fantastic", "negative" and "cranky". If he will persevere, however, he will find that it is at least no more fantastic than the extreme "subjective idealist" view that an object, such as the moon, does not exist when no one is looking at it. After more reflection the student may come to see that Shankara's outlook, though more frankly dependent on "intuition" as a source of knowledge, is by no means less credible than many Western systems; though this is not, of course, evidence of its truth. Moreover, although this again is no proof of its soundness, those who accept Shankara's view, so far from being eccentric recluses, are often exceedingly efficient in the practical affairs of life. They are certainly not negative; whether they are cranky is a matter of opinion.

Coming now to Shankara's view on the sources of right knowledge, it is important to note than Shankara did not advance any new doctrine of his own; his philosophy was an exposition—and to some extent a codification—of the traditional utterances of the Upanishadic sages. For Shankara, the Hindu scriptures were of superhuman origin, and their authority was valid absolutely in matters outside our physical experience; they expressed the mind of God. He accepted conception in the mind and perception of "outside" objects also as sources of knowledge; but these sources have their limitations and cannot lead man to that reality which is the goal of all right knowledge.

Because he relies so much on scriptural authority, however, it must not be thought that Shankara denies the validity of reason. The role of reason, however, is limited. It cannot establish truth. It can only establish relations and examine the veracity of propositions. Reasoning cannot be carried on without propositions. But every proposition is itself established by reasoning from some other proposition or propositions. These propositions in turn must have been derived by reasoning from others. Thus we are faced with two alternatives: (1) to pursue an infinite regress, which in the end is more or less bound to lead to reasoning in a circle; or (2) to admit openly that some propositions are in the nature of axioms, which cannot be established by reasoning, and which, if valid, must owe their veracity to some other source. In fact, we "know" that there are such axioms—in particular the axioms regarding the reasoning process itself. For instance, reasoning proceeds on the axiom, among others, that if there are two inconsistent propositions one of them must be wrong; the truth cannot be self-contradictory. This axiom clearly cannot be established by reasoning, because it is the very condition of reasoning and is presupposed by it. Shankara's comment is characteristic: "Those who attempt, by means of ratiocination, to realise knowledge which reveals the ratiocination itself are such great souls as would burn fire itself by means of fuel."

In the philosophical use of the term, therefore, Shankara is not a "rationalist". He does not, for example, try to establish the existence of God by the sort of arguments used by mathematical philosophers like Leibnitz, who argued that "necessary facts", such as that the internal angles of a triangle add up to two right angles, could only be explained on the assumption that there were thoughts in the mind of God. According to Leibnitz, all propositions led back to propositions of this sort, which seemed immediate and "perfect" and gained no increase in certainty by repetition, and thus qualified as a special class of truths, for which God's understanding was the only proper abiding place. Shankara does not adopt this approach at all; he recognizes straight away that reasoning leads back to axioms that cannot be analysed or explained by reasoning.

Shankara had already noticed in his day that the rationalist thinkers came to inconsistent conclusions. "All the disputants who believe in final emancipation or liberation assume that it is achieved by right knowledge; and this right knowledge, because it refers to a reality which exists, must be uniform. But those who seek the ultimate reality by sheer ratiocination hold views that are divergent from one another and mutually exclusive: The sophist establishes a system only to have it rebutted by a cleverer one. Reality cannot be made dependent on the cleverness or length of tongue of debaters. The Veda, as contrasted with their systems, is eternal and infallible." We shall see later what Shankara means by "eternal" and "infallible".

On the other hand, Shankara was not an "empiricist". He did not consider that observation, even when aided by reason, was sufficient to establish a true account of reality in our mind. It is a matter of universal experience that our sense perception often serve us badly and present a distorted view of the world "out there". Take, for instance, the fact of our seeing the sun rise every morning in the East, and travel through the sky, and sink down in the West in the evening. We "know" that the sun does not move through the sky in this way, but we cannot help seeing it appear to do so.

Again, is the orb of the sun as small as our eyes would have us believe? To argue that by further observation and experiment we can ultimately get at the truth is beside the point, for we then introduce means other than direct observation plus ratiocination. It is true that ratiocination may be used to establish relations between the things observed—as in the techniques of mathematical physics—but this is a different kind of ratiocination from that postulated by either the rationalists or the empiricists. It is, in fact, what is usually called "inference". The propositions of pure mathematics are usually regarded by rationalist philosophers as being a **priori** knowledge; for example, that two and two make four is regarded as part of the basic content of the mind and of the universe—though one's attention may be drawn to this proposition by noticing that two sheep and two sheep make four sheep. The more complex relationships between things, such as the motions of the earth and the sun referred to above, are clearly not part of the mind's furniture. Equally clearly, they cannot always be directly observed. Empiricism, therefore, is not enough.

But Shankara is not anti-rational. Reason as applied to the facts of experiment is to him an indispensable means in the search after reality; but reason has to be employed only as the tool of intuition, as a critical weapon for testing raw assumptions. Even the scriptures are not exempt from critical examination; they, too, must be rational, and Shankara is at pains to show that they are.

Perception is also valid in its proper field. "As no authority is equal to the eye in the perception of forms, so there is no authority outside of the Vedas on knowledge destined to realise that which is beyond the perceptive faculty," is how he states his position. In those realms of enquiry that are open to perception and inference, scripture is reckoned as unimportant. Scripture must also conform to the observed facts, which bear the mark of certitude through direct experience: even scripture has not the right to say that fire is cold. "The purpose of the scriptural text is not to alter existing things, but to reveal them as they really are."

In the traditional view in which Shankara was brought up, the Hindu scriptures have an absolute authority—not because a personal God wrote them or inspired individuals to write them; but because they embody the fruits of the spiritual insight of many sages who had searched for ultimate truth with single-minded devotion. They are, so to say, the fruits of many practical religious experiments, all of which have yielded the same result   The experience of the sages are self-certifying and call for no proof, and that is why the scriptures are, for Shankara, absolute, needing no external proof or support. It follows, however, that although these recorded experiences are there to help us, we have to make the experiments again and test the conclusions for ourselves. They show us the way, but we must prove by walking in it ourselves that it really is the right way.

When Shankara says that the scriptures are eternal and infallible, therefore, he means no more than that they contain incontrovertible truth valid for all time, and that they are impersonal and so not vitiated by the proclivities and predilections of lay human beings. The insight of the sages is available to anyone who undergoes the necessary training—in particular, if he carries out faithfully the duties imposed on him by the scriptures, is unselfish, and seeks to know the supreme Deity or Brahman with a steady and unwavering persistence. "A knowledge of reality as it is—reality which is quite unfathomable, but on which man's final liberation depends—cannot even be distantly guessed without the help of the scriptures. For ... this is something not falling within the ken of direct perception, because there is no colour or other qualities in it; and not within the realm of inference, because there are no features in it for inference to lay hold of."

Claiming absolute authority for the scriptures did not make Shankara's task any easier; for the Upanishads bristle with paradoxical statements, and sometimes, on the face of it, flat contradictions. Sometimes the tendency seems to be pantheistic, sometimes theistic: sometimes it is monistic, and sometimes dualistic. In some passages, Brahman, the ultimate reality, the one without a second, is regarded as something quite beyond human understanding and devoid of any qualities by which it could be described. In other passages, the Brahman is the repository of all perfect qualities—infinite, eternal, immutable, omniscient, omnipotent and omnipresent. In some contexts the universe is called a "creation" of Brahman, but elsewhere is regarded as beginningless and uncreated. Nevertheless, the underlying unity is there, and it is a measure of Shankara's greatness that he had not only the sharpness of intellect, but also the insight, required to give consistent philosophical statement to the voluminous material he had inherited from the saints and sages of his tradition.

A great many of the apparent contradictions in the Upanishads disappear when one applies the distinction between "lower" and "higher" knowledge which Shankara developed—between scripture, ritual observances, and intellectual study on the one hand, and the sheer intuitive power by which reality is apprehended on the other. Until the last vestige of "avidya" or ignorance is removed, however, it is not possible for man to conceive of a Brahman or reality without qualities. As long as he has to live in the world, man must use any tool which comes to hand to achieve his own liberation. His finite mind cannot contain the infinite, but he can use that mind as a thorn to extract the thorn of ignorance embedded in the Self. The point of the first thorn is the "lower" knowledge, which teaches in relative and worldly terms the relation of the world to the ultimate reality conceived as a God with qualities, who is a symbol—but within man's conceiving—of the indescribable Brahman without qualities.

The portions of the Vedas that lay down ritual and provide prayers and hymns were regarded by Shankara as lower knowledge intended to guide away from their sensual lives those who have relatively dull intellect and are weighed down with desires and lust; while the Upanishadic portions contained the higher knowledge intended to enlighten those who had renounced carnal desires and achieved some measure of "one-pointedness".

The lower knowledge is not to be despised, or regarded as a concession to the ignorance of the mob. In other contexts, we are glad to make use of this sort of aid. For example, a rower imagines his blades to be against fixed posts on the bank so as to reduce his tendency to "slice" the water, and he would not take any notice of criticism that he was the victim of a delusion. If symbolic worship is a sin, then so is childhood, when we are bound to learn at first by over-simplified pictures. The personal god (Ishvara) gradually brings the individual

man to realise that the individual Self and Ishvara and
the limitless Brahman are in essence the same thing.

The Western student may well pause at this point. This
view of a personal god is a very different one from the
Christian view of Jesus Christ or of the Trinity, each person of which is conceived as having attributes, though
being in another aspect incomprehensible. Organised
Christianity teaches in effect by means of what Shankara
would call "lower knowledge". But neither Christian nor
Hindu lower knowledge is derived by Hindus; for it, too,
leads to the higher knowledge of the mystics, of the unknown author of the "Cloud of Unknowing", of the blessed John Rysbruck, of Jakob Boehme and of William
Blake as also of Shankara himself.

It should be added that it is part of the traditional
Hindu attitude to philosophy and religion that one cannot transcend the lower knowledge by ignoring it. Everybody who hopes to reach the heights has to start at the
bottom and rise step by step through the lower to the
higher knowledge. And when he has "arrived", the wise
man will not "unsettle the minds of ignorant people."
But it is his duty to help those not so far advanced as
himself, to purify their conduct, strengthen their moral
fibre, and sharpen their intellect; he must lead them rung
by rung up the ladder of truth, so that they in turn may
preserve the ladder for others to follow.

What then are the qualifications which the student must
have before he may enter on the study of the higher
knowledge? They are: (1) discrimination between the
"things seen that are temporal" and the "things unseen
that are eternal", (2) indifference to the rewards of labour and to pleasure (even heavenly pleasure), (3) moral
preparation—including such qualities as peace, self-re-
straint, renunciation, patience, deep concentration and
faith, and (4) earnest longing for liberation.

It will be noted from this syllabus that moral virtues
are valued, and practised, not because they are the com-
mands of a personal deity, but because they deepen the
intuition and are a precondition of the search for spiritual ends—ends which, although they are blissful and
everlasting, are not sought as a reward for good works

by the ego—or even for the "soul", in the Christian sense —but as ends in themselves, as part of the scheme of the universe. There is no obvious reason why disinterested love and self-control should deepen one's intuition, but all the sages, Eastern and Western alike, have found by experiment that it does.

The Western philosopher may be tempted to regard this as a sadly empirical—perhaps even a superstitious—approach to what he regards as one of the great intellectual studies. Practically all Western philosophers of all schools have worked on the tacit assumption that intellectual processes alone can discover truth, and the more conservative have reacted to the influence of the accepted religious and political beliefs of their time by trying to justify this "lower knowledge" by pure intellectual processes. Hegel found it convenient to prove that the Prussian militarist state was the ideal form of Government. Bishop Berkeley was more or less bound to provide in his philosophy for a personal God not too far removed from the conception of the deity he was expected to expound from the pulpit. This is the exact opposite of the attitude of Shankara and other Indian philosophers, who have frankly regarded specific religious dogmas as a ladder to something higher.

In Shankara's view, the student must apply himself to his study with his whole being, not merely with his intellect. The cranky dilettante who dabbles with entertaining speculations and loves "always to hear or tell some new thing" will not come thereby to liberation. Philosophy for Shankara is not intended merely to satisfy intellectual curiosity, or to serve as a training in dialectic. Nor is a philosopher one who can talk "about" philosophy, or who knows the scriptures by heart; but one who has learned by intuitive experience, which is possible only when philosophy is lived.

The spiritual part of the student's training consists traditionally of three parts: (1) study of the Upanishads at the feet of a spiritually qualified teacher, (2) reasoning within oneself, and (3) meditation. Submission to a teacher who is himself "liberated"—however repugnant to the individualist Western student—is a **sine qua non** of success. There is a fair analogy between the study of philosophy (in Shankara's use of the term) and the persuit of athletic sports. If we want to row or play tennis, we are prepared to subject ourselves to an expert teacher, and we are not offended if he bellows at us through a megaphone or abuses us whenever we make a bad stroke. How much readier we should be, therefore, to sit at the feet of a wise teacher who will guide us in difficult spiritual exercises, which, if we persevere, will bring us to a state of pure bliss. The Western student will find the simple logic of this hard to accept. It does not mean that reading is valueless—otherwise this book would serve no purpose—but it does mean, frankly, that full entry into the mystic life is impossible without the initiation by a competent teacher. "Learn wisdom," says the Katha Upanishad, "at the Master's feet; for the path is as hard to tread ... as the edge of a knife." Those who have reached a certain stage learn that the submission in itself is a help to the study, because it helps to kill out the "ego", the self-interest which clouds the intuitive vision. The student need not fear that the teacher will "lade him with burdens grievous to be borne". He will know how much the student is ready to receive, and the student can always leave off if he feels that the higher knowledge is not yet for him. Very few, however, who have seriously set foot on the path do, in fact, give up.

The second part of spiritual training—reasoning within oneself—is not for the purpose of independently establishing truth, but only to remove doubts arising in the mind regarding the views contained in the revealed texts —and in particular for ironing out in the mind apparent inconsistencies. The object is to "turn knowledge into conviction".

The third part of spiritual discipline is sustained meditation upon the identity of the individual Self with Brahman until the identity becomes immediately felt. This is not a subject which can be explicitly described. It can only be experienced.

The Self

A convenient point at which to begin on any philosophy is its view of the external world. The "commonsense" view is that there are "real" objects "out there" in the world, and that these objects possess qualities—shape, colour, smell etc.—which are perceived by our "mind" through the medium or our sense organs. This view seems unassailable until we examine it closely. It is challenged by practically all philosophies, Eastern or Western—at any rate in the crude form stated above. It is also challenged by scientists, who see a table, for example, as mostly empty space peopled by a mass of moving molecules themselves consisting of atoms, which again are mostly empty space. To a scientist a table is not in itself brown: it gives off rays of a certain wavelength which fall on the retinae of our eyes and produce reactions which are transmitted by the nerves to the "brain" and "there" interpreted as a brown colour. Of course, this analysis takes it for granted that the various parts of the perceiving mechanism—the eye, the nerve fibres, and even the brain, are "out there", at any rate insofar as they belong to other people. In other words, it is necessary to adopt the commonsense view in order to prove it wrong. As Shankara puts it, we have to use a "thorn to extract the thorn". How far the final result is valid is settled, for Shankara, by experience, and it is enough to note here that an element of intellectual doubt is bound to remain after practically any refutation of the commonsense view.

It is part of the commonsense view of the world that each of us exists as a separate individual who is "conscious". In a certain sense, all that "I" see—the earth, the trees, the stars, other people,—is "in" my "mind". On the other hand, my "mind" is, in the commonsense view, situated somewhere inside my body, which moves about in this world of earth and trees, and stars and other people. In short, my mind is in the world, and the world is in my mind. How are we to solve this puzzle?

It is not purely verbal. To attempt a solution, we must try to answer such questions as: What is my mind, and exactly where is it? What does the word "I" mean? Is it my body, my intellect, my "soul", or what? Where, for example, do "I" go when "I" am asleep?

To understand Shankara's view of the self, we have to realise that for him the word "I" can have four different meanings: though these four meanings are not entirely separate and distinct. "I" can denote: (1) the inner consciousness, or knower; (2) the "antahkarana", or "inner organ"; (3) the ego; (4) the "jiva", or soul.

We shall deal in detail with the last three of these aspects of the person in later chapters. It should be mentioned here, however, that the thing which is reading these lines and trying to grasp the ideas now being described is primarily your "antahkarana", gentle reader, and in this book the words "I" or "we" mean the antahkarana" unless we expressly say otherwise. The antahkarana is, so to speak, the material, thinking, perceiving mind—a physical thing with parts and attributes. With this crude, clumsy thorn, the student is invited by Shankara to extract the thorn of avidya or nescience and "realise" his inner Self.

What is this inner Self, with a capital S, and how do we know that it exists? The answer can come only from direct intuitive experience. Every person at some time or another has a glimpse of the inner Self—even if all his life he is far from being "liberated". It may be in a time of great fear, or on a peaceful summer evening. The body may be in good health or at the point of death. It may come after study, or after reading a beautiful poem, or after seeing a suppurating wound. It may come when no particular outward events are happening. But whatever the cause, the experience is the same. The inner Self contemplates calmly the whole activity of the person. It is as if we stood outside ourselves, without passion, without thought. For the moment, all our busy imaginings are quiet, and the Self, the knower, looks at what we usually regard as ourself, at the ego, its faults and virtues, as if it were another person. No writing or study can by itself bring the student to the knowledge of the Self, and if he has at present a repugnance to the whole idea, he had better stop here: his time is not yet. There are psychological techniques which help, but the will must first be there; if it is not, then the student is not yet ready to grasp Shankara's philosophy.

The Self is indescribable; if it could be described, it would not be the Self. The whole of this chapter—and, indeed, of this book—can therefore be nothing more than a series of different springboards from which the reader must dive himself. On the logical level, the most that can be said is that the Self cannot be disproved. It is sufficient to pose the question to realise its absurdity. No one can say "I am not." The most that can be said is that this transcendental Self is the real subject in all experiences —whether of sorrow, pleasure or disappointment —and it remains unchanged as these experiences come and go; it is the string which runs through the multi-coloured beads of the ever-changing content of experience.

It is interesting to set this statement in contrast to the popular view of Eastern Philosophy as "negative" or "life-denying", to use Albert Schweitzer's term. Never-theless—and this paradox is characteristic of the whole Eastern approach to philosophy—the Self can better be understood by looking at things which it is **not**—so much that one Upanishad, in pointing out the way of holiness, says in its enigmatic fashion: **Neti, Neti**—"Not this! Not this!"

In the first place, the Self is not the ego. The ego is a physical thing with attributes. Twenty years ago, I—that is to say, my ego—was irritable and touchy, now I am more mellow and tolerant. Then I was jealous, now I have learned better. To be able to stand outside oneself suf-ficiently to make such statements presupposes—whether one likes it or not—a "knower" who surveys the ego and notes its changes, its faults, and its decay—"my memory is not so good as it was". The mental states which make up the ego are objects in relation to the pure Self. We enhance the comparison between the Self and the ego by transferring qualities of the body and the senses to the Self—as when one says "I am "fat", "thin", "blind" etc." The ego is admittedly the subject, and the "outside" world the object, vis-a-vis the ego, but "that which cognizes both subject and object is the supreme Self itself. Neither of them can know it. That alone can know clearly which is neither subject nor object". In short, you cannot get to know your inner Self in the way you can get to know the personality of somebody else.

The Self is not a "soul" or spirit—a sort of spook which leaves the body at death. In Shankara's philosophy, the soul or "jiva" is the Self as conceived by the antahkarana or material mind. In fact, it is what the reasoning mind without the assistance of intuition makes of the Self. The jiva is the Self immanent in the material mind, but it is not itself the Self. There is no "soul" which exists as a separate entity in its own right.

The Self is not the antahkarana or material mind, although this is perhaps the nearest to the commonsense view. More will be said about the relationship between the Self and the antahkarana in the next chapter. It is sufficient to say here that the student who could realise the Self, so far from exerting his busy discriminating faculty, is called upon to still the evermoving flow of thoughts, relax the mental sinews, and loose apart the bonds of the ego and all its little anxieties.

If the Self is not an individual soul, it is also not a collection of individual souls—a sort of world soul—for the Self has no individuality or manifoldness or limitations and admits of no divisions. The individual self or person bears to the pure Self the same relation as the space within a pot bears to universal space, and its limitation —like the limitation of the space within the pot—is illusory. It is a reflection of this impartite quality of the pure Self and its one-ness with God that the words "Atman" and "Brahman" are employed synonymously both by the Upanishads and by Shankara. It is true that it is possible to discern, albeit dimly, a slight distinction between the two terms. Brahman is used where the transcendental aspect of the Self is meant, the Creator; and Atman when we start from the person and think of that person's Self as a manifestation of the Deity and thus involving the universe. Brahman is the universal aspect of the Self which needs to be revealed; Atman is the self-revealing essence deep within us. But to the enlightened person, Atman and Brahman are known to be the same. The problem that the mind contains the world and the world contains the mind is solved when this identification is intuitively known.

The Self is not, of course, the body. Shankara regarded consciousness and matter as two different orders of reality. Admittedly, consciousness may be found only in association with matter, but although it is true that where consciousness is, the body also is, the converse is not true; for in a corpse in which all the several organs of the body are still intact we find no consciousness. Consciousness is not an essential property of the body, or of any matter—as such. Consciousness can comprehend matter, but matter cannot comprehend consciousness. One who has eyes can either look or close his eyes and pretend blindness; but a blind man cannot see at all. Nor can consciousness be identified with the senses. Were it so, there would be as many selves as there are senses, which would make impossible the self-identity which we already know intuitively. If, on the other hand, the senses are really one single perceptive element which constitutes the self, then we should have the simultaneous enjoyment of sight, sound, taste, feeling. But our inner Self can contemplate these entities separately and knows them to be so.

The consciousness may be likened to a fire, and the body and senses to wood. If there is fire, the wood may burn, but if there is no fire, the wood will not burn. The combustion in the wood is not seen to exist in the fire, but we think of it as derived from the fire, because it does not occur unless the wood is touched by the fire.

There have, curiously, been philosophies that have denied the existence of any real self at all. Some Buddhists regarded the self as nothing more than a series of psychological states, which create the illusion of a permanent self—just as a flame on being revolved creates the illusion of a continuous circle. Shankara's reply to this was a direct appeal to the intuitive notion of self-identity. Momentary flashes of ideas—however similar—may explain the illusion of continuity, but the facts of identity

A.S.—2

and memory—so that I can say: "It is I who had before **me yesterday this very book** which is before **me now"** —are not to be explained away. But for the persistence of a conscious Self, through and beyond time, no such relations, comparisons and contrasts are possible.

To the school of Buddhists who regarded the whole world as an emptiness, a total illusion, Shankara retorted that one could say anything with one's tongue in one's cheek, but the mere fact that there were persons to devise the idea of such a void presupposed that the void contained something. While this is not a disproof of the Buddhist position, which is logically very difficult to disprove, Shankara's reply makes it equally obvious that it cannot be proved. Its analogue in Western philosophy is in the extreme form of subjectivism known as solipsism —the view that our mental states are the only things we can know, and that there is therefore no reason for supposing that anything except ourselves and our mental states exists in the universe. This is very hard to disprove; it is equally impossible to prove, especially if one accepts the extension of this view developed by Hume—namely, that the self is non-existent and that only the mental states exist.

If we may digress for a moment, it is interesting to note the arguments with which Hume demolished the self. First, he denied the facts of introspection. He asserted that if one looked within one found only images, feelings, passions, but never the self—only "impressions" Secondly, he argued that experience consisted of "impressions" and "ideas" with an independent existence. He believed that all that any knowing mind could know would be these impressions and ideas. The impressions were fleeting and could therefore not be the objects of, or give rise to, a continuing self.

In the days of Shankara there was also an idealist school holding similar views to Hume's. Shankara's reply to this was that the entry of the idea of reality into the mental states and the attempts made by the mind to interpret such a reality presupposes that the reality exists. This reality is the pure Self which, we know, intuitively can and does contemplate and illumine the mental states. Mental states, like the flames of candles, cannot illumine themselves. " 'My mind which was wandering has now been steadied.' Understand it thus: 'I am he who knows this activity of the mind'." If there were no reality apart from the different states of the mind, all knowledge would be the product of the ever-changing attitudes of the mind, and knowledge would cease to have any validity or certitude. The view that all knowledge is relative is self-stultifying. Hume himself was not, of course, convinced by his own arguments. In the last analysis he regarded them as showing that the Self could not be established by reasoning—a view which Shankara would heartily have endorsed.

The Self is not an inferred object in the sense, for example, of the "substance", which Locke devised to act as a "support" or substratum for the world as we perceive it. Nobody can **experience** this substance; it was brought in, to put it bluntly, to fill a logical gap: to give uniformity to simple ideas of heat, taste, colour etc., which were regarded in Locke's theory as giving rise to ideas in our minds, which "represent" qualities in the object itself. Western philosophy is much addicted to these purely logical entities, about which William of Occam is reputed to have warned his pupils by the tag **"entia non multiplicanda praeter necessitatum"**. It would be a great error to suppose that the various entities referred to in this book—the jiva, the antahkarana, etc.,—are merely intellectual concepts brought in for the purpose of making a coherent metaphysical system. The student can become aware of the existence of these entities by direct intuition—that most convincing of all sources of knowledge. Shankara, indeed, rejected the proposition that the Self is an inferred object precisely on the ground that, if it were, it would contain an element of doubt which attaches to all inferences, and an experiencing person would doubt whether it was he or another who was having an experience.

To end this catalogue of the things which the Self is not, it is not an **attribute** of consciousness. For either the Self must be the same as consciousness or it must be distinct from it. If it is the same, it cannot be an attribute.

If it is distinct, then there must be something relating the self to consciousness, and that something would in turn need two more relations, one to link it with the consciousness and one to link it with the Self, and these two relations would need two others, and so on. The whole conception of logical relations is irrational. The Self is not an attribute of consciousness because it is consciousness itself.

The Self is not the body, the ego, or the soul, nor is it a series of mental states or a logical postulate. What is it, then? It is impossible to describe or define it. It does not have qualities or parts or attributes. The Self is not established by proofs of its existence; it is prior to all proof. It is not possible to deny the existence of the Self, because it is the very essence of him who doubts or denies it. It cannot be grasped by thought; it has to be grasped whole with the whole being.

The most important property of the Self is that it is directly revealed, or if, owing to the inadequacy of language, we may use the word in a double meaning, it is self-revealing; and its immediate revelation is the source of its certitude. But owing to avidya, there arises a confusion when we search for it. "The Self, which is ever with us, appears, owing to ignorance, as if it were unattainable; but when that ignorance is removed by knowledge, the Self is attained."

The Self is the basis of all knowledge, for nobody can say "This is known, but there is no Self". The reader need only advance this proposition in regard to the reading of this book to realise how absurd it is. But, one might argue, it is possible to get lost in the sight of a glorious sunset or in a captivating novel—one can "forget oneself" in these things. A little reflection will reveal, however, that the proposition contained in this conventional phraseology is absurd. If it is possible for me to "forget myself" in some act which I perform—in other words, if it were possible for me to experience something otherwise than in relation to my conscious self—upon the termination of the experience, "I" should not be sure whether it was to me or to someone else that the experience had occurred and was subsequently remembered.

It is the ego one forgets—and a very good thing too.

There are no circumstances in which we can say the Self does not exist. Even in deep sleep, when all the perceptive faculties are quiet and there is no consciousness of any objects, the Self is fully and completely present. This is demonstrated in that on waking from sleep the subject never doubts that it was he who slept. It cannot be maintained that the subject merely **inferred** that he had slept, because no such inference is possible unless something at least very similar had occurred in his experience. "Sleep" would indeed have no meaning for me unless I know that I am awake and that sleep is an event in **my** life.

The Self is sometimes described in Sanskrit as "sat, chit, anandam", which means approximately "absolute existence, absolute consciousness, absolute bliss". The Self, the thread which runs through the beads of temporal experience, is beyond the temporal. No limit—spatial or temporal—restricts the Self; it illumines and transcends all limited things, whether they are physical objects, mental concepts, or pure abstractions. That which apprehends limitations must necessarily be above limitations. S. Radhakrishnan says: "We cannot be conscious of a limit unless we are conscious of what is beyond the limit. That which is altogether limited or finite cannot know itself as limited or finite. The idea of the unconditional is distinct in nature from all other concepts and so cannot be derived from them". The Self is unlimited and eternal, and as there cannot be two such beings in the universe, it is said to be "one without a second".

The "one without a second" is of the nature of pure consciousness. "That Atman is throughout consciousness; consciousness is its exclusive nature, like the salt taste of a crystal of salt." Consciousness and existence are inseparable.

The Self is also absolute bliss. All happiness and unhappiness in the worldly sense are fractional or inverted manifestation of the beatitude of the absolute Self. Only avidya veils and perverts this beatitude. Every desire and striving of every being has the manifestations of the Self's beatitude for its end. No object is desired for its own sake but for the sake of the Self. In the Brihadaranyaka Upanishad, Yajnavalkya declares, "Not for the sake of husband or wife, mother or child, brother or friend, is each object dear, but for the sake of the Self within; but this pure bliss of the Self is not realised until the veil of avidya is lifted." The Self here denotes not the ego but the supreme Self. A pre-condition for lifting the veil of avidya is to live a life of "unselfish" devotion to others, and to mortify and kill out the ego.

The Self is permanent, unlimited in time. If we argue that our consciousness is perishable, this presupposes that there is a consciousness which is conscious of its perishability and which is therefore permanent. We, as knowers, are present in all our knowledge and experience, and do not undergo the changes which the knowledge and experience contained in our consciousness undergo. The knower can affirm: "It is I who know now what exists, it is I who know what existed in the past, and it is I who will know what will exist in the future"; but, while the objects of his knowledge vary, the knower himself is un-varying, for he is in the past, the present and the future, the essence of him being eternally present.

Let us now return to the point with which this exami-nation of the Self began namely, the nature and validity of our knowledge of the "outside" world. This problem has given rise to the most diverse opinions among Western philosophers. To put the matter in an over-simplified way, the "idealist" schools have mostly maintained in one form or another that "we" have no knowledge of "outside" objects as such. The "mind" perceives only "ideas" or "representations" of those objects obtained through the senses; and the "ideas" themselves are not of physical objects, such as tables, but of **qualities**— heat, blackness, squareness, etc. A corollary of this is that objects cannot be said to exist unless they are per-ceived. When I went out of the room just now, the fire which was burning in the grate went out of existence, and when I came back, the fire came back into existence —burned down a little maybe!

To avoid such conclusions, the "realist" schools have maintained that the objects "out there" exist, though we may not perceive them as such. We perceive their quali-ties (e.g. heat) as sense data (sensation of warmth), and we go out to the objects, so to speak, and fill in their real character by inference. A blind man may have to do a great deal of inferring from what he perceives by touch.

The discripancies between these two schools — and the many intermediate schools — are probably traceable to circular arguments tacitly introduced into the wording of the propositions; but however this may be, they are the products of the antahkarana, the reasoning mind, trying to analyse its own relations with the outside world by purely logical methods. It is trying to lift itself by its own—boot-straps. According to Shankara, the distinction between subject and object is purely illusory. The inner Self contains and pervades both subject and object, which seem to the antahkarana to be separate only because the inner Self is veiled by avidya. Shankara took the idealist view to the extent that he considered that objects had a purely **relative** existence, and he agreed that if, for example, I say "I feel pain", the pain is not distinct — except verbally — from I (the antahkarana), and the quality of the fire producing the pain is also ultimately indistinguishable from "me" as a subject: it is "in" me as the pain. "I am not Mandu but a cramp" is a literally correct statement.

Where Shankara parts company with both realists and idealists is (a) that he regarded what we normally regard as subject and object as being both contained in a Self which was neither subject nor object, and (b) that he regarded the Self as pervading both subject and object — as both immanent and transcendent.

Another important difference between Shankara and all the materialist and realist schools is that he regarded the view which distinguishes the objective world from the subjective world at all as an illusion. This sense of distinction, Shankara says, is due to avidya and calls it "conventional" — valid only for one state of our consciousness.

One may argue that if the Self is all that is, and subject and object are really not distinct, it is impossible to explain the ordinary experience of the self as "here", enclosed in the body, and the object as "there", in the world outside. Shankara answers that the Self is not only within the body but without also. It pervades everything knowable in the same way as it pervades the body space. It is "here" as well as "there" and externality is unknown to it. The very nature of apprehended space does not admit of a division on the basis of here-there-ness or in-out-ness. Take again the example of the pot. The space inside the pot seems to be enclosed within it, and we call it the space "within" the pot as opposed to the space "without" the pot. But this division is a fictitious one, for the pot — i.e. the walls or sides of it — which seemingly cuts up space into inside and outside parts, is itself in space. In like manner, the body is in the Self, and is only perceived through avidya as bounding the Self so as to exclude everything else as not-Self.

Yet if the Self comprehends everything, if it is omnipresent and omniscient, how is it, one may legitimately ask, that all objects everywhere, in past, present and future, are not always simultaneously experienced by the Self? Why do they appear and disappear in the Self's experience from time to time and place to place? Shankara says that this appearance and disappearance does not happen to the true Self but to the Self as perceived by the antahkarana through the veil of avidya. "There are two kinds of vision: that of the eye, which is ephemeral, and that of the Self, which is eternal. Similarly, there are two kinds of hearing. And there are two kinds of knowledge: external and internal."

The view of the Self set forth by Shankara — and indeed his whole philosophy—is not confined to the Hindu religion or to any race, or class or time. Religious teachers and others of the most varied backgrounds have come to this view. In general, the rather verbal, logic chopping approach of the Western "school" philosophies has not been a fertile ground for this kind of philosophy. Of European philosophers, Berkeley seems to have been groping for the view of the Self which Shankara adopts. Although in many way a solipsist, he believed, with praiseworthy inconsistency, that the mind had an inherent "notion" of a real self—although in other contexts he denies the existence of a priori knowledge of this kind.

"What I am myself," says Berkeley, "—that which I denote by the term I—is the same with what is meant by **Soul** or **spiritual substance.** But if I should say I was nothing or that I was an idea, nothing could be more evidently absurd than either of these propositions— ... In a large sense, indeed, we may be said to have an idea or rather a notion of **spirit.**"

In Christianity one also finds a sad preponderence of the dogmatic and ritualistic over the mystical and spiritual. But something very like Shankara's view of the Self is contained in the idea of the "Kingdom of God" taught by Jesus, by seeking which "all things shall be added unto you". He did not fail to explain that the "Kingdom of God" is within you.

The great Christian mystics, approaching the question from a great distance in time and doctrine from Shankara, expound, sometimes implicitly but sometimes in open terms, the exclusive reality of the Self. St. Catherine. in "Vita and Dottrina", says: "My me is God, nor do I know my self-hood except in God".

A tradition in Islam quotes Mohammed as declaring: "Whosoever knoweth his own self, knoweth his God." The Sufi philosopher, Hafiz says:

> Self-knowledge is the only pearl
> In the sea of life;
> Like whirlpools round our self we whirl
> In incessant strife.

A Sufi hymn reads:

> I am none else than Thou, and Thou than I.
> I am Thy body and Thou art my Soul.
> Let no one say hereafter that I am
> Other than Thou or Thou other than I.

The mystic vision is denied to no person and to no age or time. Jew and Gentile are on the same footing. Whatever the precise dates of the Upanishads and the sacred books of China, it is certain that they are all very ancient. It was at least some five centuries before Christ when Lao Tze said: "There is an infinite being which was before Heaven and Earth. It lives alone and changes not. It moves everywhere but is not affected...That Tao is of the essence of all...The wise man knows no distinction". And his disciple Chuan Tze said: "Your life is the delegated harmony of God".

The Greeks in the midst of their syllogisms had true knowledge. When Socrates asked the Delphic Oracle what constituted the highest knowledge, the answer was, "Know thy self".

Perhaps the matter may best be summed up by a modern teacher, the Swami Vivekananda in India, who said, "Buddhas and Christs are but waves on the boundless ocean which I am".

Epistemology

How can we come to know the Self? The answer is that if we truly know anything at all, it is the Self; and everything else we seem to know is a product of avidya or nescience, which splits up the pure or integral knowledge into subject and object. For if the Self is universal and is the only reality, then, it is not the real that calls for explanation, but the false, the erroneous and the unreal.

Why should avidya exist at all? Is it ingrained in the Self? If so, the non-dualist concept of the Self would be destroyed. If it were altogether outside the Self, it would have to bear some relation to the Self — a type of relationship which, as we saw in the last chapter, is unreal.

Before we can get any further with answering these questions and understanding the nature of avidya itself, we must look at Shankara's analysis of the antahkarana and the part that it plays in the perceptive process through which we derive our empirical knowledge: in Western terminology, we must consider his theory of psychology.

Here we encounter a fresh difficulty in the exposition of his philosophy. As we have said before, in talking of the Self we are trying to explain something which by its very nature cannot be split up into bits and "explained", but can only be intuitively grasped as a whole. Shankara had to deal with this difficulty in teaching his philosophy among the intellectual philosophies of his own day. In his analysis of the antahkarana, he was dealing not with a spiritual entity, but with what we may for a moment loosely call the "mind". He was in the territory which the "school" philosophers did, and still do, rightly regard as part of their province, and he was compelled to take notice of the theories of his time. This makes much of what follows deceptively familiar to the student of Western philosophy and makes it essential for him not to forget two important things: (1) The propositions are intended to be no more than a counterpart on the intellectual plane to

Shankara's whole view of life. Any similarity between them and the views of Hume, for example, is coincidental: Hume just happened to hit on the same argument 1,000 years later in the same limited context: in other respects, the views of Shankara and Hume are on different planes. (2) Shankara would not have regarded the arguments themselves as proving anything particularly valid. He was aware of the limitations of this sort of reasoning, and, no doubt, with the clear insight of a liberated sage he "felt in his bones" that the arguments are to some extent circular: he produced them to meet the challenge of intellectual philosophers. We must therefore warn the student that he will not get any nearer to the essence of Shankara's philosophy by analysing, criticising and construing the arguments set out in the latter part of this chapter.

The antahkarana is, so to say, the "material" mind; and it is the seat, not only of intellectual processes, but also of feelings. It is not, however, a kind of sense organ, because it has on its own level a direct perception of itself and its own changes. The senses are the tools by which the antahkarana apprehends objects. If it is not in a state of attention, the senses do not function. We may have a thing in front of our eyes and still not see it: we aptly say "My mind was somewhere else".

The antahkarana is neither infinitely large nor infinitesimally small. It is usually thought of as pervading the body and thus being about the same size: not gross and solid like ordinary matter, but an ethereal, transparent, shining thing in which objects are manifested, as it were, in a mirror. This power of the antahkarana is not, however, inherent in it: it gains this power through its association with the Self. In the Self we "Live and move and have our being". In another metaphor, the Self is "reflected in the ethereal element of the antahkarana and, like the sun, reveals the entire world of matter".

These metaphors are at best merely rough indications of what is intended; the exact nature of the interaction between the Self and the antahkarana cannot be expressed in words. An example in which a similar difficulty occurs, but is calmly accepted, can be found in music. As a matter of scientific fact, the vibrations per second of the higher note of a perfect fifth are exactly one and a half times those of the lower note. From the strictly musical point of view, the essential thing is that the fifth has a characteristic "bare" sound, which every person with a reasonably musical ear can recognise. Now, the knowledge that the two notes were separated by a perfect fifth could be obtained by a musician, if he were also a physicist, by measuring the rate of vibration of the two sounds separately and comparing them (indeed, a tone-deaf person also could do this with the appropriate apparatus). The musician can, however, tell by ear alone that it is a fifth. This fact that he can get the same knowledge on two different planes, does not lead him to question its validity on either: he accepts that a certain kind of noise is "associated with" a vibration ratio of 3:2, but no amount of analysis will ever disclose the nature of the association. This is an analogy to the interaction of the Self and the antahkarana in the process of perception of the world. The ideas run parallel, and they interact, but they do not coincide, because they are on different levels. In the normal process of knowing, the antahkarana splits the Self up into three: the subject who knows, the object known, and the process of knowing or cognition. The Self is seen in the mirror of the antahkarana, and it is a principle of our constitution that the mirror should be a distorting one; we "see through a glass, darkly".

The antahkarana is ever active and assumes various forms or "modes" — except in deep sleep, when its activity is latent in itself. One of its modes is the consciousness of itself, which may be called "ego-hood". The ego commonly confuses itself with the real Self. When we say "I am restless", we mean that the antahkarana is restless, but we wrongly transfer the restlessness to our inner Self. Herein lies the essential difference between mere introspection and the knowledge of the inner divine Self, which comes from knowing this philosophy as Shankara knew it. Knowing his philosophy and knowing "about" it are on two different planes.

When the antahkarana assumes the mode of doubt or indetermination, it is called "mind" — in the sense used in the statement "I cannot make up my 'mind' ". The item "mind" includes resolution, sense-perception, desires and emotions. When the antahkarana has the mode of certainty or determination, it may be called "intellect", including the powers of judgment and reasoning; and when in the mode of reflection and remembrance, it may be called "attention". The ego, the mind, and the intellect function only intermittently; their activity has a birth, growth and death. An argument, for example, begins with the premises and works through a chain of reasoning to a conclusion. "Attention", however, may endure; and this mode of the antahkarana is regarded as the most important, because meditation, contemplation and concentration belong to its province, and these are the activities by which a person uses his antahkarana to seek and find Reality. They are the point of the thorn used to extract the other thorn of avidya.

It is an essential function of the antahkarana that when acting as an instrument of perception it not only perceives objects but determines our reaction to them. To this extent, it is a sort of mental counterpart to the nervous system of the body. Professor Deussen says that "the assigning of a common organ for mind and conscious will, and a common function for ideas and resolves, corresponds to the psychological fact, according to which the brain both shapes the impressions of the sensible nerves into ideas, and also carries into execution these ideas so far, as they become resolves of the will, by means of the motor nerves." This does not mean, of course, that the concept of the antahkarana is necessarily valid. The antahkarana is a psychological and not a physiological entity, but the parallel which Professor Deussen drew is suggestive. It is a parallel which we might well expect to find.

The antahkarana is not, however, a purely philosophical concept. It is not an entity invented to meet some logical or formal difficulty—like Locke's "substance", which was introduced because one could not have ideas in nothing, or the "luminiferous ether" of the nineteenth century scientists, who could not contemplate light waves in nothing. The antahkarana is regarded as a real object by Shankara which the student can detect by direct experience.

The interaction of the inner Self and antahkarana is essential to the functioning of the antahkarana. Shankara does not say on the one hand that the antahkarana can know itself, as the materialists openly or tacitly do contend; nor does he say on the other hand that "spirit" (i.e. the Self) and matter exist in two separate water-tight compartments. Both these theories lead to ludicrous conclusions. The materialist theory, taken in conjunction with the determinist view which logically accompanies it, is self-stultifying. If the mind is a machine, both (1) the proposition that it is a machine and (2) its consciousness of itself as such a machine are inevitable products of the machine itself, and therefore have no validity—though it is fair to say that equally they are not **necessarily** false.

The second theory—that spirit and matter exist in water-tight compartments—leads to a difficulty that confronted Aristotle: it is difficult to assign appropriate areas to teleology (his conception of spirit) and matter without violating the unity of "reality". If spirit influences matter, is its influence a spiritual or material influence? If it is a spiritual influence, matter must have a spiritual aspect. If it is a material influence, then spirit must have material properties. Descartes regarded mind as disparate from matter, but to get them together for psychological purposes, he had to invent a fluid which he called "animal spirits"!

Shankara's approach to this basic problem is quite different. In the first place, there are in his view three entities to be accounted for—(a) the pure Self, (b) the antahkarana, and (c) the body and other matter. The essential interaction was, for him, between (a) and (b), whereas the Western philosophers have been looking mainly at the interaction of (b) and (c). For him, the apparent incompatibility of the pure spirit or Self and the antahkarana was not real but only empirical: ultimately, both of them are in essence the non-dual Atman. He says frankly that the Self contains the antahkarana, and the antahkarana reflects (though it does not contain) the Self. If this view seems inexplicable and contrary to commonsense, it is no more inexplicable than the relationship between the two aspects of a musical fifth, and no more contrary to commonsense than such theories as Descartes'.

On the theory of perception—which is in effect the relation between the antahkarana and matter—Shankara had not himself worked out any well-established theory, but it may be interesting to set out briefly the ideas developed by his school, and particularly by Dharmaraja, who lived about 1600 A.D.—almost contemporary with Descartes. These views are not a part of Shankara's own teaching, but they show the way the Vedantist mind has worked under his influence.

Broadly, the Vedantist view is that the antahkarana "streams out" of the body through the senses and comes in contact with the object. One part remains within the body, another gets in touch with the sense object, and a third or "modal knowledge" connects the two. If the ego is then illuminated by the pure consciousness, perceptive knowledge arises. Merely directing the sense organs does not in itself cause perception: the activity of the antahkarana is indispensable: otherwise we stare at an object without perceiving it. The "mode" of the antahkarana and the object are not perceived as two because both occupy the same space—even as the pot and the space within it are located in the same spot.

In perception, the object and the antahkarana must both be present. This distinguishes perception from memory, which is a recollection of past perception. Inference is distinguished from perception in that there is no contact of the antahkarana with the object inferred. For instance, in inferring fire from smoke, the antahkarana is in contact with the smoke and the connection between the smoke and the fire is only recognised from memory. In memory, we have the Self associated with the past experience determined by the antahkarana. In recognition, we have perception and the memory of past perceptive experience fused together.

The later Vedantins also held that it was necessary for perceived objects to be suitable for being perceived. Virtue and vice are attributes of the antahkarana, but they cannot be perceived in the sense in which a chair can be perceived. The Vedantins also drew a suitable distinction between perceptions effected through the senses and perceptions not effected through the senses. A book is perceived through the senses of sight, touch, etc., but pleasure and pain are not perceived through the sense organs.

But to return to Shankara's own theory of knowledge The antahkarana plays an important part in his epistemology: for, as we have seen, it is the antahkarana that creates individuality by an illusory splitting up of the non-dual Self into the self and the not-self. The Self as associated with the antahkarana appears in two aspects: (1) the Self as immanent in the antahkarana—the "spark divine" or Atman in the "deep heart's core" of each one of us; and (2) the Self as the transcendent Spirit or Brahman, but conditioned by the operations of the antahkarana. To be brief and also to avoid misunderstanding through misleading translations, let us call these aspects S^1 and S^2. Relatively to S^1, the antahkarana is an attribute; relatively to S^2, it is a limitation. In other words, S^2 is a limited conception of the universal Self generated by the antahkarana. Empirical knowledge is a mode or posture of the antahkarana as illuminated by S^2. It is this illumination which confers the validity which we all instinctively ascribe to intellectual processes. The processes might go on without the illumination, but they would not be conscious processes.

The modes of the antahkarana being subject to constant change, there arises, as S^2 constantly illuminates these changes, the delusion that S^1 is also subject to constant change. In other words, the ego is mistaken for S^1. It is like saying that the sun itself is quivering, when we see it reflected in the ripples on the lake. Shankara says: "Though the body, the senses and the mind carry on their respective activities only by their dependence on the conscious "Self", yet, owing to non-discrimination (avidya), the qualities and activities of the body, the senses, the mind, etc., are attributed to the Self, that is pure existence and pure consciousness, in the same way as blue colour is attributed to the sky."

One of the difficulties that have bothered Western philosophers is the explanation of this sort of error. The difficulty is a serious one, because on almost any view—whether "commonsense" or "philosophical"—error seems to enter to a greater or less degree into both perception of events and judgments about them. True, the problem is not so bad for the idealist philosophers, because they maintain that the "mind" (by which they mean in effect the antahkarana) never makes contact with outside reality at all; it merely knows "ideas", which at most are "representations" of what goes on outside. We do not see a table: we merely experience some impression of browness, solidity, coldness, etc., which are really in ourselves. On this view, it is always possible for the mind's judgment on its own ideas to be at fault. But the realist view, according to which the mind is pictured as a searchlight playing on a real object outside ourselves and reporting on what it finds, does not provide for error. If the mind is really in contact with a real thing, there can be no mistake about what the thing is.

Shankara's view was that all errors in perception are located in the antahkarana. The error arises through a mistaken attribution or transference of ideas.

For example, the perception of silver where there is only a silver-coloured conch shell is explained as follows: When the senses come into contact with the shell, there is a modification of the antahkarana with reference to the shell. The illuminating Self (S^2) then shines on the shell itself and on the antahkarana so modified. At the same time the person's avidya is awakened, and, working on the recollection of real silver (which is, of course, revived by the similarity in appearance between the silver and the shell), it causes the impression of silver to be attributed to the real Self (S^1). So it comes about that the ordinary earthly personality can be at fault, but the real Self is not touched or sullied by the false attribution of the error to it—any more than the sun is defiled through shining on a forgerer.

Errors due to physical defects in the antahkarana—such as defective eyesight due to jaundice—are similarly explained, although in this case there is no need to assume the specific intervention of avidya. In all perception and in all human judgment, however, there is always some element of limitation or error due to false attribution (adhyasa). Dreams are also illusory perceptions. They are not mere memories; for in a dream one says to oneself, "I am talking to a beautiful woman", and not, "I remember talking to a beautiful woman". Dreams are different from waking perception, but the difference is one of degree and not of kind. The shell that remains after the erroneous silver has been seen for what it is, is in neither case the ultimate "ground"; there is always the supreme unity, the Self, the Brahman. The Western student may compare this view with Kant's threefold division of things into the "phenomenon" (the shell), our representation of the phenomenon (the silver), and the "thing-in-itself". To Kant the thing-in-itself was unknowable; but to Shankara it is the ultimate ground of being, the Self, and is accessible to direct intuitive experience.

These explanations should not, however, be taken too literally or pressed too far. They are themselves empirical theories and have their limitations; in the ultimate analysis, all errors and illusions are inexplicable. If the silver did not exist here and now, it could not have been perceived: nor could mere memory have accounted for it, for when we remember something, we are really recalling a past perception of an object that is no longer present. But if the silver really does exist here and now, we should be able to pick up silver and not shell. So the silver perceived is neither real nor unreal. It belongs to a third category. Thus, of error and illusion we can only say that they exist and we know that they exist; but in saying so we imply that though we fall victims to error and illusion we are in part beyond and above them. The purpose of philosophy—in the sense in which we apply it to Shankara's teaching—is to bring us into a realm of Reality in which error and illusion no longer exist.

How, then, does illusion arise at all? We can only say that it is the product of avidya. What is avidya? Avidya is the empirical form of another concept called maya, for which there is no equivalent English term. Whence, then, maya? That again is inexplicable for the same reason that illusions are inexplicable. The student is entitled to ask what use there is in embarking on an explanation of something inherently inexplicable, if that inexplicable is to be explained in terms of another inexplicable. The only answer is that the final inexplicable, maya, provides us with a fundamental principle that underlies the infinite variety of errors and illusions. Maya, in the famous Upanishadic metaphor, is the clay from which the jugs, plates and pitchers of errors and illusions are made. But the very process of explanation is illegitimate when we discuss ultimate reality, because explanations involve chopping reality up into bits and establishing relations between them—a process which is itself invalid.

To summarise: Shankara taught that there are three orders of reality—(1) the absolute, (2) the empirical, and (3) the apparent. To the apparent belong all illusory perceptions, including dreams; to the second order belong all empirical perceptions; to the first order the cognition in which there is neither subject nor object, nor mediation of any kind, the Self alone illuminating itself.

Nobody is in a position to throw stones at those who deal in inexplicables. We are surrounded by miracles all the day long—the orderly operation of our bodies, the skill with which thousands perform delicate manual operations, the mechanism by which love or anger can appear in a subtle and indescribable flash in a person's eye. Above all, there is the immensely complex and differentiated set of psychological and physiological processes by which a child becomes created as a cell so tiny that it can barely be seen by the most powerful microscope, and yet contains shut up within itself some very slight and subtle cast of countenance or idiosyncrasy of gesture which will later give it an inescapable likeness to its parents, and which by some further miracle may persist for the best part of a century. A great deal of valuable work has been done in describing the mechanism of growth and classifying the facts of heredity. The various factors in heredity have even been related in a rough and ready way to some of the parts of the individual after it has started to grow, but very little headway has been made towards understanding the miracle of the original cell, and none at all, on the scientific level towards understanding the cause—if that is the right word—of the whole process.

Most European philosophers have challenged the commonsense notion of cause and effect—or at least the commonsense description of the processes usually regarded as causal. Shankara also subjected the idea of causality to a penetrating analysis and showed that ultimately it is unintelligible.

In the first place, the causal law requires a relation between the cause and the effect, and all relations of this kind are unintelligible, since a relation is either (1) identified with one or other of the two things related—in which case it is superfluous, or (2) separate from the things related—in which case we have to look for two fresh relations connecting the ends of the relation, so to speak, with the two things related, which lands us in an infinite regress.

Shankara then refuted the various theories advanced by the schools of thought of his time—all of which have counter-parts in Western philosophy. These theories were based broadly on one of two assumptions: (1) that the effect is pre-existent in the cause, or (2) that the effect is not pre-existent in the cause but is an entirely new thing produced out of the cause. Taking the second view first, the primary difficulty is that only like causes produce like effects: one cannot sow oats and reap barley: curds must to some extent exist in milk—otherwise it might equally well be made from clay. The argument that there is some "subtle predisposing form" in the milk that produces the curds merely takes us back to the first assumption. If it is argued that a cause has a certain "potency" to produce a specific effect, this potency being non-existent until it is itself produced, it may be cogently asked whether this potency is (1) of the nature of the cause, (2) distinct from it, or (3) altogether of the nature of non-existence. If (1) is true, then the potency is superfluous. If (2) is true, then since the potency is distinct from the effect (and from all other effects) it is difficult to see how it could produce a specific effect. The third possibility would not explain the emergence of a specific effect at all. In other words it is difficult to conceive of any such potency unless it were in some sense one with the cause and also the effect.

If the effect is pre-existent in the cause in a latent form —and it cannot be in any other form—and becomes manifest as the effect after the passage of time, we are still in difficulties. What is this manifestation? It must itself in some sense have been produced, for otherwise (a) it would be eternal and all effects would be liable to become manifest at all times, and (b) it would be the one causeless thing in existence—a formidable exception to the original assumption that all effects have causes. Does the manifestation exist before it is itself manifested? It is a contradiction in terms to say so. On the other hand, if it is non-existent, we are faced with an effect that was altogether non-existent before it appeared, which is contrary to the premise from which we started. Moreover, if the effect is pre-existent "in" the cause, in what manner can the effect be said to abide in the cause? A separate "intimate relation" linking the two would, as we have seen, be unintelligible. How, moreover, would the effect which is an aggregate of parts subsist—if it is to do so —upon its cause viz., its constituent parts? Would it subsist (1) upon all the parts taken together, or (2) upon each of them singly in turn? If (1) is true, then it would be impossible to perceive a whole as such, because the theory would apply to the process of perception itself, and there would not possibly be in one act of perception a perceptive contact between the individual elements of the cause and the perceiving sense. In fact, of course, we do grasp complex wholes collectively—the notes of a chord for example.

If (2) is true, and one segment of the whole effect comes into contact with its corresponding constituent causal part, then although the difficulty of perceiving the individual elements of the cause disappears, we shall have to imagine a series of constituent parts other than those out of which the effect was actually produced, so as to make it possible for the former series of parts to subsist upon the latter series in succession; it is by a series of constituent parts distinct from those of the scabbard that the sword fits into the scabbard. Such a supposition would lead to an infinite regress, because a new series of constituent parts would have to be imagined which would reside upon the series of constituent parts first imagined, and thereafter a second new series and so on.

On the other hand, if the whole effect were to reside completely in any single one of its constituent parts, then while the whole cause is performing its function in one part, it can scarcely be performing its function in another. If the cow effect resides in nothing but the horn cause, on this view the horn would be expected to perform, **inter alia,** the function of the udder in addition to its own function, which is absurd. In a chord one note would be sounding not only for itself but for the other notes of the chord.

On this subject Shankara's logic reaches a new and finer shade of subtlety in the following passage: "Further, if the effect were to be non-existent before its origination, then the process of origination would have neither a grammatical subject nor any substantiality. For origination certainly is an action, and as such requires—like any other action, such as walking—a grammatical subject. That we should have an action without a grammatical subject is a contradiction. When we speak of a jar originating, if the origination is not to have the jar as its grammatical subject, we shall have in that case to imagine some other grammatical subject (say, potsherds). And similarly when we speak of potsherds originating we shall have to imagine something else as being the grammatical subject of that action. If that were true, when one says 'the jar originates', one will have to be taken to say that it is the potmaker and other causes which are doing the originating. In ordinary life, however, when there is a statement made about the origination of the jar, one never understands that even the potmaker and so forth are being originated: these are understood to have been already originated. If, further, we were to argue that the origination of, and the acquiring-of-a-concrete-individuality by an effect is simply the effect's coming into relation with its cause and with the genus existence respectively, you would have to explain how a thing that has not yet obtained substantiality can have any relations at all. A relation is possible only between two existing entities, and not between two non-existing entities."

Shankara argues further that the very statement that an effect is non-existent prior to its origination is absurd, for since the non-existence of an entity is void of characterisation, we cannot apply to it a limitation such as "prior to origination". "Surely an attempt at delimitation, like 'The barren woman's son was king before the coronation of Purnavarman' cannot convey any specification as to when the barren woman's son (who is void of all reality) became, or is, or will become King." Shankara concludes on a characteristic note : "He . . who considers the effect as non-existent prior to its origination: in his theory the operation of causal agencies will have no material on which to operate; for as the non-existent effect cannot be that material, it would be like using . . . a sword . . . for the purpose of hacking the ether to pieces."

The conclusion is that, however we may look at it, the causal law is unreal. The effect is in essence one with the cause. Cause alone is real, and change is only phenomenal. The cause only appears to change into effect; what actually changes is the name and form. The clay and the pot have clay for their essence; but there is a change of name and form when the pot is made. Similarly, the space enclosed in the pot may appear to be an effect of infinite space, but it is manifestly one with the cause. The change is only in name and form, which are a fabrication of avidya and valid only for the phenomenal world. The snake that one perceives erroneously where there is actually a piece of rope may be considered to be an effect of the rope, but when the cause, the rope, is known, the effect vanishes. Thus the cause alone is real. This view is not far distant from that of Aristotle. To Aristotle's view, it is often objected that the process of analysis between form and essence can be carried back indefinitely, and that we can no longer stop at the "earth, air, fire and water" of Aristotle's time, but this does not seem so serious in the light of modern physical research into the constitution of matter. At any rate, neither his view nor Shankara's is inconsistent with the results of scientific research. Where Shankara parts company with both Aristotle and the scientists is that, whereas they feel that they have come to the end of their research when they have reached earth, air, fire or electrons, or whatever they regard as the basic "material cause", Shankara saw as the "ground" or essence of all such material causes the all-pervading Self or Brahman.

Cause and effect are always presented together to our consciousness. Though we may distinguish them within the consciousness, we cannot separate them in fact. For instance, it is only the presence of the clay-cause that brings us the knowledge of the jar-effect. A good example of a cause and effect which clearly cannot be distinguished is a cloth, which is an aggregate of the constituent threads. The effect here is the cause arranged in a certain way—given a particular form and name. All that the "efficient" cause—to use Aristotle's terms—i.e., the weaver—does with the "material" cause—threads— is to rearrange the material cause into the form of the effect—the cloth. The new effect form is also one in essence with the cause, "inasmuch as what does not exist already in the cause as being one in essence with it, cannot be originated". Mere change of form cannot alter the essence of things. For surely Devadatta (the Indian equivalent of John Smith) seated with his hands and legs drawn together does not become a different entity in essence when one observes him in another position with his hands and legs stretched out ... In a like manner, our parents and relations, even though we observe them day after day in different postures, do not become different in essence, inasmuch as we can recognize them. A child in the womb is not reckoned as distinct in essence from the child that is born. We should not be misled by the manifestation of that which is latent. We cannot see the pattern of a roll of cloth until it is unrolled. The plant is concealed within the seed, the apparent concealment being due to our avidya.

In other words, neither the hen nor the egg comes first, but both stretch back into the infinite past and promise to stretch to infinite in the future. No causal explanation can ever be complete. This again is a view which has been accepted by some European philosophers and scientists. Jeans says, "There is no scientific justification for dividing the happenings of the world into detatched events, and still less for supposing that they are strung in pairs, like rows of dominoes, each being the cause of the event which follows and at the same time the effect of that which precedes".

Shankara regards the idea of a "first cause" as involving a self-contradiction because it would mean that there was a causeless cause. Nevertheless, Shankara demolishes the causal theory only to maintain the doctrine of the Self on which his whole philosophy is based. This does not mean that the relationship of cause and effect has no validity at all: it has an empirical validity in the field of material objects. It is true to say that the dog has died today as an effect of the poison it ate yesterday; what is not true is (1) that the poison and the live dog are somehow transformed into a new article, the dead dog; (2) that giving the poison and the death stand by themselves without any relation to the past or future; or (3) that the whole of experience can be chopped up into isolated events connected by causal relationships of this sort going back to some "first cause".

It is now possible to summarise Shankara's position regarding empirical knowledge. The notion of "consciousness-of-objects", which is the basis of all our empirical knowledge, is a source of error. We split up the one reality of consciousness into the subject, the object, and the subject-object relation; but no such relation is ultimately true, or even intelligible. Moreover, our knowledge of objects involves some notion of a "materiality", whose nature we regard to be in a region of non-self and non-consciousness. The consciousness of objects is the result of a confusion between the real Self and unreal objects; it is the product of "adhyasa" given rise to by avidya. An illusory perception of a thing is attributed to the real thing in itself and thus to the all pervading absolute Self. Similarly, the causal law, although it has a relative validity in relation to our empirical knowledge, is in the last analysis a fiction.

In Shankara's view, all objects existing in space and time themselves, are manifested only in relation to the Self and are all ultimately found to be either the Self in essence or nothing at all. In truly knowing anything we know only the Self; and the object-consciousness of ordinary life is true only for a particular mode of consciousness conditioned by the antahkarana.

We therefore come back to the essence of Shankara's approach. Dialectical thinking is dependent on the self-illuminating consciousness for its manifestation, but such thinking cannot bring us to a knowledge of the real. To say "I am I" is tautology and gets us nowhere; to say "I am X" is, on the face of it, absurd. This is just what we do, however, when we are thinking dialectically. This is how we perform the false attribution of outside things to the inner Self. These attributions are natural and beginningless, and are the root of all false knowledge and sense of duality.

The real is inexplicable; it simply is. In going from the unreal to the real, we jump on to another plane of thought. It is not a continuous development or a series of steps. No man by taking thought can add a cubit to his spiritual stature. And when the unreal is known, it vanishes immediately the reality behind it is perceived The process is instantaneous and there is no time lag between the two, for if there were such a gap between the superseding of the unreal and the apprehension of the real, this gap would be filled with something which was of the nature either of the real or of the unreal— and so on in an infinite regress. The real comprehends the finite, but the most which the finite mind by itself can acquire is a vague sense of the infinite reality. Thought cannot know the real.

It is this limitation which forces us to seek the real by negative rather than positive methods; otherwise we remain, so to speak, hypnotised in the state of the unreal and unable to proceed to the higher plane of the real. Right knowledge is therefore defined as that which is not nullified or contradicted by subsequent experience. Right knowledge is self-manifest and therefore not dependent on any extraneous agency such as physical light, sense organs, or even thought. Knowledge acquired is valid only until it is superseded by higher knowledge. Of course this is equally true in the empirical realm studied by science. A straight stick appears crooked when dipped in water. In relation to the eye, the crookedness is real. When touch reveals the straightness of the stick, that is relatively a higher truth.

On the other hand, because our empirical knowledge shows this sort of relativity, this does not mean that knowledge itself is only relatively true. The relativity resides in our finite minds. In science, hypotheses and theories are constantly overhauled and rejected and fresh ones substituted, not because scientific knowledge is admitted to be relative, but because we have in us an innate faith that even in this realm absolute knowledge is attainable. In the view of Shankara, the world-appearance is true to our waking consciousness, but it will be finally superseded in its entirety when Brahman, the absolute reality, is realised. Brahman is not superseded by any experience. When that which is perfect is come, that is in part is done away.

In taking this view, Shankara steered a middle course between the two main Hindu schools of thought. One school held that all knowledge—empirical or spiritual— was self-valid, self-proved or self-evident; while the other held that knowledge was only valid if it withstood certain tests such as consistency (they were what we should today call "verificationists"). Shankara held that knowledge was self-valid insofar as it was not vitiated by defect (dosha)—or what we should call "errors of observation". He argued that this purely negative test did not destroy the inherent self-validity of knowledge.

This chapter has taken us through some rather complicated by-ways of thought; and at the end we are not left with any imposing system of constructive metaphysics. This conclusion amounts to little more than that reached by Hume—that ratiocination is not in itself a sufficient means for the discovery of truth. The importance of the part of the writings of Shankara and his school that we just reviewed lies in that we can see him going over the same problems that have occupied metaphysicians from Aristotle 1,000 years before his time to Whitehead over 1,000 years after. Putting the matter at its lowest level, his conclusions point to a solution of these verbal puzzles on the intellectual level, which on the one hand is at least not inconsistent with the empirical scientific approach and on the other is a reflection of a coherent attitude on the spiritual level.

Cosmology

One of the most puzzling—and important—features of Shankara's philosophical system is his view of what we call in the language of commonsense "the external world". As we have seen, Shankara did not accept the philosophical "idealism" of the Buddhists, which is very similar to the views of Hume—the view that all that "we" know is "impressions" of "ideas" of things in the "outside world", and that we have no real self but only a succession of mental states. Shankara made no attempt to suggest that the commonsense view of the world is not correct **as far as it goes.** When an object is perceived, there is a real object before the perceiver. Even illusory perceptions—such as a snake in what is in fact a rope—have a limited reality. Moreover, in denying reality to the external world we can do so only in implied relation to something else which is undeniably real. Therefore, when Shankara says that Brahman is the sole reality, though this statement by implication denies **absolute** reality to the phenomenal world, it presupposes a **relative** reality in it. We might say (though the words are vague) that the world has a reflected or "delegated" reality from Brahman.

This bring us face to face with one of the basic problems of all philosophy; if Brahman, the transcendental Self, is perfect, how can it be the creator of, or even associated with, a world which we know intuitively contains what we regard as imperfections, or at least, contradictions. It may be, of course, that the imperfections are either in ourselves as perceivers (which Shankara did not accept) or in our ego or senses—in the outer layers, so to say, of our personalities; but in so far as other people are part of the external world for me, their imperfections are imperfections in that world so far as I am concerned. Therefore, in one form or another, the imperfections are located in the external world. Shankara was not content to postulate a separate devil or Satan who was responsible for creating the world, or endowing with evil and imperfections a world already created.

Now, in Shankara's view, if objects are to exist at all they can do so only in relation to a consciousness which apprehends them. The vast number of objects in the universe, and the constant but orderly changes among them, compel one to assume an infinite, omniscient, omnipotent mind to apprehend them. This mind, which reckons the entire universe as its body, is caled the "saguna" Brahman or Ishvara—the Self "with qualities". The saguna Brahman is the "nirguna" Brahman, or the Self "without qualities", when it is associated with the universe as comprehending it.

The view set out above is subject to the vagueness and imperfection of all terms when we get near to the core of the philosophy. On the face of it, Shankara's view is not so different from Berkeley's—that the moon would cease to exist when nobody is looking at it, but for the fact that it is always a thought in the mind of God—but Shankara's conception of a thought and of what was "in the mind" of God were different from Berkeley's. Berkeley's God was essentially a person outside the universe; Shankara's God was conceived as not personal at all in the ultimate analysis, and he (or rather, it) was involved in all parts of the universe though not identified with them.

It is interesting to note in passing that the Buddhists of Shankara's day held virtually Berkeley's view, for which there was a technical term, **drshti-srshti-veda** (an approximate equivalent of our "subjective idealism"); and that Shankara categorically denied it, in terms somewaht reminiscent of Dr. Johnson's kicking a large stone and saying of Berkeley "I refute him, thus". Just as we are conscious of ourselves, so are we conscious of things "out there". Moreover, when the subjective idealist speaks of something "in" his mind, which is in himself, he tacitly accepts the validity of the notion of extension in space, and once extension is admitted it is difficult to deny the existence of objects, which to the commonsense view are extended if they are nothing else. When Shankara denies reality to the world, he is not taking up the subjective idealist position. The unreality in the world is seen only in juxtaposition with the Absolute. It follows that Shankara did not accept the Buddhist view that the mind itself was unreal as an entity, and that the world was no more than a dream. He argued that a dream is superseded when the dreamer wakes, but no waking experience is afterwards sublated in this way.

When Shankara speaks of a "first cause" or director of the universe, it might be thought that he was adopting something like the "watch" argument of some Christian apologists, that a watch implies a watchmaker, but this would be a misunderstanding of Shankara's position. In one of his commentaries he refutes all the various doctrines designed to establish through logic, reason and inference the existence of God as the efficient cause and director of the universe. Broadly, his approach is that the facts of astronomy, for example, may **suggest** that there exists something majestic behind (and within) the universe, but that that something cannot be inferred from those facts. Reason can at best only construct a sort of concept of a super-man with a super-humanly acute reasoning power, but such a super-man would be wholly "within" the space-time framework. He himself would need a material body in order to create the universe, but since the only place where material bodies are observed is in the universe itself, creation would be impossible for a deity conceived in this way. Moreover, the "watch" type of argument presupposes the ultimate reality of the chain of causation, which, as we have seen in the last chapter, Shankara did not accept.

How, then, does Shankara approach the problem of establishing the existence of Ishvara—the nearest thing in his cosmology to the personal God of Christianity? The answer is that he does not really treat the matter as a philosophical problem at all. He recognised from the beginning that for all but the most nearly liberated souls the direct frontal approach to the impersonal nirguna Brahman was virtually impossible. The ordinary man needs the support of a warm and personal loyalty to some tangible manifestations of God—a Saviour who binds up the broken hearted and carries the lambs in his bosom, and gently leads those that are with young; who will support us all the day long of this life and give us peace at the last. To many men and women those conceptions are the staff of strength to which they cling, not only in the overwhelming torrents of war and pestilence, but in the everyday erosion of poverty, illness, and the sense of being housed in an animal slowly dying without a purpose; and in that peculiarly odious disability which besots this age of anxiety—the sense of not belonging anywhere.

Shankara did not, therefore, reject the God portrayed in the scriptures of his race and creed. The main intention of the scriptures is to teach the higher, the nirguna Brahman, but side by side with that they teach the saguna Brahman, which still has every perfection, which is still above evil and falsehood, which creates, sustains and dissolves the universe, and which is at once both its "material" and its "efficient" cause. The scriptures recognise that merely repeating "I am Brahman" cannot by itself destroy ignorance and take us to the highest Reality any more than a clerk can become a managing director by saying "I am the managing director". Until we perfect our knowledge on the empirical level of the saguna Brahman, we cannot come to the nirguna Brahman, for it is quite beyond our ordinary ken. We shall not see it until we burst out of the bud of empirical knowledge into the flower of absolute knowledge. Ishvara is the mediator between our conditioned jivas and the unconditioned Brahman.

Putting the same thing in another way, we cannot arrive at Reality by ignoring or by-passing avidya. We must first of all comprehend ignorance and error and transcend them. To do so, we must reflect and cogitate over the nature of the unreality that surrounds us. But we can contemplate the nature of the unreality only if we have before us in juxtaposition to the unreal that which is real. Ishvara is, for Shankara, the proper object of such contemplation. It is interesting to recall here that Evelyn Underhill said that the act of intuition by which she came to know God—the nirguna Brahman in Shankara's terms —was "not specifically Christian"; yet in the godly life

A.S.—3

which she led thereafter she belonged to a highly ritualistic religion and delighted in images of saints, and cribs
and such.

The incarnation of God in which Shankara believed
was that set forth in the scriptures of his time. He believed in Ishvara because the scriptures revealed him. But,
like many Christians, he also argued that the Vedic statements were true because they were revealed by Ishvara,
who is omniscient. This is a circular argument and does
not prove anything—although equally, of course, it does
not mean that either of the two statements is untrue.
Shankara did not, however, regard the Vedas as valid
wholly or even mainly because Ishvara revealed them,
but because they are impersonal and objective. A more
detailed account of his views on this subject is given in
Chapter II: we need only repeat here that his view is not
inconsistent with reason, but in the end it is made valid
to us only by the intuitive knowledge which all the sages
have possessed, and which we, too, can have if we are
willing to submit ourselves to their disciplines. Its validity
does not rest on the authority of any earthly individual
or organisation.

We will now give a brief account of how, in the Indian
cosmology, the universe is built. There are superficial
resemblances to some modern scientific theories, but
these resemblances are accidental. The whole structure of
modern science—that enormous scale model showing how
the wheels of the universe turn—was not available to
Shankara. This does not mean that his theory of creation
is more or less sound than those which have been built
up against the background of modern science. The philosopher begins where the scientist leaves off, and the
sage knows that what they both express are aspects of
a unity, which he knows without the intervention of observation or inference.

The substance out of which Brahman creates the universe is called "maya", the final inexplicable which we
noted in the last Chapter to be the ultimate basis of the
error inherent in all human observation and judgment. It
is for this reason that maya is sometimes translated as
"illusion", but this word carries misleading implications.

Maya is in a sense the creative power of Brahman, who, in association with maya, dominating and yet conditioned by it, is Ishvara, the Lord. Maya is not a substance existing apart from Ishvara. There is not really a relationship between them in any ordinary sense. Maya is, so to say, an "aspect" of Ishvara, bearing the same relationship to him as energy bears to the energiser or heat to fire.

Maya is to be inferred from its power and the effects it produces. These are twofold—the power of creation and the power of veiling. Its power of veiling is not preponderant or absolute, but comparable only to the small patch of cloud which veils the orb of the sun, which has a diameter millions of times the size of the cloud itself. The cloud itself, however, is made visible only by its revealing the nature of the sun. In its aspect as a veil, maya gives rise to avidya, which, as we saw in the last chapter, is the source of error in man.

Thus, in the Aristotelian terminology, the Brahman, which is pure consciousness, may be conceived as the causal agent or "efficient cause" when the emphasis is on its nature as pure consciousness underlying all created things; and it may be conceived as the "material" cause when the emphasis is on its energy in its aspect as maya. The simile often used to illustrate this two-fold aspect of Brahman is that of a spider, which when it weaves a web may be regarded as the efficient cause of the web, but insofar as it supplies from its own body the saliva for the web, may be regarded as the material cause of the web.

The theory of creation is that Ishvara creates the world and after a vast period of time reabsorbs it into himself. After it has been reabsorbed, his power of creation (i.e. maya) remains for the time being absorbed in him. After a short pause, there is an outburst of new creation. This process goes on from beginningless time to eternity.

There is a systematic theory of inorganic nature. In broad outline the first creation is "akasha". Then follow the other four elements—air, fire, water and earth. Akasha is the subtlest of all elements and is filled with an extremely attenuated form of matter. From akasha arises air, from air fire, from fire water, and from water earth. In dissolution, the process is simply reversed.

These elements are not to be understood in a modern scientific sense. On the other hand, they are not merely outmoded or superseded science; they represent a different way of looking at the same phenomena as are studied by scientific methods, which reveal the structure of matter and energy and how the gross forms of matter behave—even how matter and energy are inter-related—without finding out what matter and energy really are. One cannot look to scientific method for more than an analysis of fine structure and a description of the way things work; and in this respect the Hindu philosophers of Shankara's time were neither better nor worse situated than we are to speculate on the origin and real nature of the world. It requires only the elementary scientific knowledge called "commonsense" (with which Shankara was liberally endowed) to see that there is order and unity in the inorganic world, and the modern analysis of matter into electrons, protons, neutrons and other absolutely identical and featureless units has merely provided additional evidence of this unified substratum of the general order—including apparently diverse chemical elements—sodium, gold, etc. In a rational world such as Shankara envisaged we should expect to find such a substratum.

The difficulties begin when life enters on the scene. In Shankara's view, however, there was not that rigid distinction between living and dead matter and between the various sorts of living matter that commonsense—and until recently, science—has assumed. In the Hindu theory, the human organism is forged out of the three elements, earth, water and fire: the antahkarana out of earth, the "prana" or vital organ out of water, and "vak" or speech out of fire. Inorganic nature serves a special purpose of its own. Organic nature consists of body mechanisms into which souls enter, and produce four classes of living beings—gods, men, animals and plants. This material world is the field in which the individual souls operate and realise their desires and ambitions and the rewards of their actions.

Man is distinguished from plants and animals in that he has not only the growing-power of the plant-world and the moving and sensing-power of the animal world, but also the powers of reasoning, determination and discrimination and willing. Men who use their powers with discrimination and realise their good ambitions turn into gods. Even plants have living souls: they, too, are fields of operation and are tenanted by souls in expiation of their sins.

Most theories of cosmology have to cope with the conundrum with which we began: "How is it that the Lord, who is good and perfect, would create a world which contains evil and imperfection?" and, more cogently, "If God sustains the world and absorbs it back into himself, is not his perfection sullied by the imperfection of the world?" This is closely linked with the conundrum as to how God can be both immanent and transcendent —at once outside the universe (which apart from him must contain everything—and if he isn't "in" the universe, where is he?) and at the same time indwelling in the hearts of men or elsewhere in the universe. These conundrums are probably more verbal than real, and there are probably concealed circular arguments in them. In particular, how does the person posing the conundrum know that the world contains evil? Surely it is because he has in himself an idea of what is good? But where does he get his idea of what is good? And what distinguishes good from evil? Surely from his inner consciousness, from his Atman? If he denies the existence of the Atman, then it is hard to see how he can give any account of the origin of his ideas of good and evil, or indeed describe the distinction between them. And if he denies the existence of the Atman, there cannot surely be **for him** any problems relating to the immanence of God?

These conundrums also occupied the minds of philosophers in Shankara's day, and we will now give some idea of his attitude towards them. They are not soluble by dialectic, and the most that dialectical analysis—such as the elementary example given above—can do is to reveal the artificiality and largely verbal character of the problems themselves.

In the first place, the theory of creation set out above does not convey that Ishvara is immanent in the various bits of the universe. In other words, Shankara's philosophy is not what among European philosophers would be called a "monistic" one, though this term is often incorrectly applied to it. If the world (the effect) were a modification of Ishvara (the cause) the world would exhaust Ishvara, and by comprehending the world, we should have comprehended the entire Reality. There would be no room for liberation in such a scheme. Moreover, the world is subject to change, whereas Ishvara is changeless. Nor is the world a part of Ishvara, for the infinite has no parts. Ishvara, in Shankara's view, remains unaffected and unsullied by the impurities of the world, which is only a product of his energy, maya. Creation does not imply any desire on the part of Ishvara, which would detract from his self-sufficiency and perfection. Just as when we are concentrating on an absorbing game of chess and have no extraneous desires to appease, or when we are breathing without conscious effort, so does Ishvara create the universe. Creation is his nature, and all things created are the outpouring of his supreme joy. He is not affected by his creation any more than a conjuror is affected by the results of his illusions. In another metaphor, Ishvara is like, a magnet, which, immutable itself, can alter the properties of iron with which it comes in contact. This does not mean that Ishvara plays an irresponsible game with his creatures. Towards those who exert their free-will and seek him he "means intensely and means good"; they find him and are filled with joy.

Nor is it inconceivable that a cause like Ishvara, which, although, strictly speaking, it has no qualities, may be said to be analogous to a sentient being, should create inorganic insentient stones, since the human body does something analogous to this in growing hairs and fingernails. To the question whether the world, which is essentially impure, would not at the time of its reabsorbtion into Ishvara sully his pure nature, Shankara answers that the clay in its effect-form as a plate may be classified into good, bad and middling quality, but that when the effect-form returns to the cause, it does not import into clay the impurities of its effect-existence. (These are not, of course, dialectical arguments; what Shankara does is to cite analogous cases in which it does not occur to us to put forward objections; it is thus suggested to us that the original objections are in the nature of special pleading based on words and not on things).

Shankara also answers the objection that if Brahman is the sole reality and is also immutable, the subject-object distinction in the world should not be possible. Deva-datta, who eats rice, would insist from the commonsense point of view insist that the rice he eats is different from himself, Shankara's reply is that the distinction between subject and object, between cause and effect, is largely unreal. Foam, waves, ripples and bubbles all appear to be distinct from one another, and yet their essence is one and the same ocean. He quotes from a famous passage from the Chandogya Upanishad: "By knowing one lump of clay you know all things made of clay, the modification being only verbal since the clay alone has any reality ..." Jars, plates, or water-pots are no more than clay-in-essence. Reality belongs to them only because they are of clay.

Shankara is not even prepared to concede that Brahman may be one-in-essence like a tree but having more than one nature—just as the tree has many branches, leaves, fruits etc.; nor does the immutable Brahman undergo modifications like Devadatta standing and moving. On the contrary, to use another metaphor, in spite of changes that take place in the form of a human being between childhood, youth and old age, we identify the person as being the same. Moreover, a man is looked on as father by one, brother by another, and uncle by a third, without altering his essential identity as one person. A woman does not change her identity when she changes her name on marriage.

Try as we will, however, words cannot smooth over the false distinction which words have largely created. From the standpoint of ultimate truth there is no scope for the ideas of "inside" and "outside" the universe, controlling, being controlled, creating and being created, and even omniscience. Brahman, camouflaged by maya, "assumes like an actor" the forms of the various effects from the Creator of the universe, Ishvara, right down to a gnat or a fly or an atom. And, therefore, "inasmuch as the entire world is at once an effect of Brahman and nondistinct from it, the solemn Vedic injunction—by which what has not been heard becomes something already heard, what has not been thought becomes something already thought, what has not been known becomes something already known—is fully ratified".

We can now return to the problem of the origin of "evil"—by which most people mean (a) pain and disease, which seem to be "imperfections" in the material world, and (b) ill-will and hatred—especially in other people!—which offend against our innate sense of what is fitting and seem to many people an imperfection in our moral make-up. A good deal of our ideas on what is "evil" is often traceable to threats to our beloved ego. A murderer who practises on some foreign dictator seems almost virtuous, whereas one who practises on ourselves seems a depraved wretch. An influenza epidemic is not seen as a triumph for the influenza germ, but as a defeat for man, the most important creature in the universe. It is fairly certain that if by prayer and meditation a man could divest himself entirely of his ego—and thus of his anxieties about its welfare—he would cease to notice the existence of "evil" either in himself or in others. To put it bluntly, however, it is impudence to question the Creator's wisdom in this matter. It is a part of us and of the world as he has made it that the facts should be as they are, and of our destiny that we should, at some stage in our spiritual path, think some of them evil. Moreover, if "evil" is inexplicable, so are the wonderful earthly joys which are showered on us without our deserving, or even asking—love of our mates, of children, of beauty in Nature, and a thousand more.

Shankara's view was that the Lord should be looked on as rain, which is the common cause of wheat, oats and barley. The rain makes it all grow, but each grows in its own way. The Lord does nothing without consideration; there is no capricious cruelty in him. In the long run, over the whole sequence of a person's rebirths, the Lord metes out rewards and punishments to each according to his deserts. This implies a view of sin which is wholly foreign to those brought up in the Christian tradition, in which it is an essential thesis that we have each only one lifetime and that salvation and the redress of "evils" is a matter for a second life in Heaven (or Hell), and is not entirely determined by merit or demerit but mainly by faith in the power of a vicarious sacrifice. The Hindu believes that advancement in the spiritual life is solely a matter of one's own efforts. All individual souls will ultimately attain enlightenment, and they advance or recede from the goal according to their efforts and their behaviour.

The virtue earned by a soul in one incarnation stands it in good stead when it begins again; but vices and backslidings have to be expiated. All evil-doing has to be paid for—indeed, is paid for at once, because the doer loses ground immediately, in that he falls further from the blessed goal of being reunited to his Creator. It makes no difference that outwardly he may appear to be flourishing like the green bay-tree. This is the doctrine of "karma"—a very difficult notion for the Western mind to grasp. The word covers approximately the entire range of deeds from the potential to the actual in any being. It does not carry the pejorative overtone of "sin", but it is something more than material cause and effect. Our past "karma" is **now** inevitable, but it is not "fate" in the Greek sense, for we can always influence the future. No success is certain or "comfy"; but no failure is beyond repair. We shall consider the ethical implications of this view in Chapter IX.

If this view of "evil" is accepted, the problem of the origin of evil seems far less cogent, but it gives rise to another. If karma, as an entity, got into the universe—or was put into it by Ishvara after the beginning of creation —and if it is karma in turn that determines that men shall be born and reborn, are we not in the fallacy of mutual dependence neatly called in Indian dialectical parlance "kunda-badara-nyaya"? (A person who has forgetfully left the kunda (pot) under the badara tree, on being questioned about his kunda says, "I left it under the badara tree." He is then asked where the badara tree is, and says, "It stands over the kunda"). This difficulty would be real if the world was created, so to speak, with a bang. Only if we assume a beginning for creation in space and time (and when were **they** created?) need we seek for the origin of karma.

In fact, is Shankara's view, the series of births and deaths has gone on from eternity, every transmigratory existence depending on the nature of a previous one. In other words, the whole question of a beginning for creation, maya, as well as for karma, is an illegitimate one. The entire idea of causality, relation, birth, death, etc., is relevant and legitimate only for the logical propensities of our finite mind. To speculate on the beginning of the world while we are within the world is like a child in the womb trying to speculate on the age of its mother. There cannot be a beginning in time and space for something which is the cause of time and space. Beyond the mind, these problems do not exist at all. To seek a First Cause is to be like the little man in the film cartoon who wanted to take the salute as he himself marched past. The problem of creation arises only in the empirical aspect of the world, where the answer is unknowable; from the point of view of reality, the problem is inconsequential.

An objection which is sometimies raised to the worldview held by Shankara is that if Brahman the creator is identified as one in essence with Atman in human beings, it seems irrational that he should fashion such a prison-house as the body, with its attendant pains, fears, old-age and death, and then enter it himself. Shankara's answer to this is that the transcendental Self in its aspect as Creator is not entirely the same as the Atman. The transcendental Self remains unaffected by its own creations, while the embodied soul, out of ignorance, imagines that it is harried by the miseries of the universe. Once the embodied soul realises its oneness with the transcendental Brahman, it ceases to have any idea of Brahman as its creator, "inasmuch as that right knowledge wipes out all kinds of dealings-in phenomena, which are just a pageant set on foot by false knowledge". In other words, the conundrum we started with does not exist for and cannot be formulated by a liberated soul. As Shankara puts it: "From the point of view of the liberated soul, where is the creation, and whence can there be defects such as evil-doing? This transmigratory world which gives rise to these notions of ill-doing is an erroneous perception based upon failure to discriminate between the Brahman and the limiting adjuncts, consisting of this whole assemblage of bodies and organs, which are the fabrications of names and forms and themselves the product of avidya. From the point of view of the highest truth of all, the world has, as we have said again and again, no feal existence. The feeling of the 'I' as being the subject of birth, death, cutting, piercing and the like, is a delusion, as these events belong to the body only."

This does not mean that the world is not real — as experienced; the world has this relative existence as long as avidya exists, but when avidya is destroyed by the advent of the consciousness of Reality, the world becomes unreal. But just as the reality of the world is not absolute, so also its unreality is not total, like a barren woman's son or a square circle. It cannot be said of it that it is, or that it is not. The negation of the world stretches into both the past and the future. When avidya is destroyed, the world is found never to have existed, and it never will exist; for when the illusory silver on the shell is realised as shell, the illusory appearance of silver not only vanishes but also gives rise to the knowledge in which that silver illusion never existed and could never exist thereafter in that context. "As soon as consciousness of non-duality arises in us," says Shankara, "the transmigratory state of the individual soul and the creative quality of Ishvara vanish at once, the whole phenomenon of plurality which springs from wrong knowledge being superseded by perfect knowledge."

One last objection. Is it not possible that the whole process of the negation of the world is itself a false entity — a delusion? And if it is not a delusion, is it not a positive and real entity itself — thus contradicting its own hypothesis? Shankara's answer to these questions is that the process of negation of the world-appearance is not different from, but identical with, the process of apprehension of Reality. Negation involves not only the negated world-appearance, but the negation itself; both disappear at once and the Real alone remains. Falsehood and truth are not contrary entities such that the negation of falsehood or the falsehood of falsehood will mean truth. Only relative truth may be contrasted with falsehood. "The silver appearance is false" is not the statement of an absolute truth: the silver appearance is false **in relation** to the shell: and the shell, relative to the false silver-appearance, is true. Thus only if we hold the world phenomenon as a partial truth or falsehood in the setting of the absolute Reality can we accept the falsehood of falsehood as true. In the realm of total Reality, the total falsehood of the world is not nought.

It would be possible to continue this chapter to great length without getting any nearer resolving the conundrum we started with. Western philosophy has provided a large number of different answers, all more or less tentative and smelling strongly of circular arguments. Eastern philosophers — including Shankara — seem to speak with two inconsistent voices at once — at any rate, when they are (as they must be in treatises) in the realm of reason and exposition. Western philosophers try to "solve" the problems, to find intellectually satisfying verbal answers; Eastern philosophers teach a way of living and believing, the object of which is to enable the student to see intuitively the unreality of the questions, and to grasp how Brahman can be both immanent and transcendent, the world both real and unreal, both perfect and imperfect, created but beginningless, and our lives a dream but also "broad waking". Only when avidya is overcome, can we achieve this. Book learning and reasoning will take us only part of the way. "For we know in part and we prophesy in part. But when that which is perfect is come, that which is in part is done away..... For now we see through a glass, darkly; but then, face to face: now I know in part; but then shall I know even as I also am known."

Maya And Avidya

In the last chapter we said that the personal deity Ishvara has produced the material world from the pure impersonal Brahman by the power of maya. It is now time to look more closely at this concept of maya. We have seen that the association of maya with Brahman goes back to beginningless time; that its relation with Brahman is that of energy to energiser; that it has two powers — the power of creating, and the power of veiling and thus causing error, from which it has acquired the rather misleading name "illusion". But what is maya?

It has to be said at the outset that maya defies our power of logical understanding and rational comprehension. It is neither real nor unreal: neither positive nor negative. It is inexplicable and indefinable. It is the illusion in the perception of silver where there is actually only a shell, and that deeper illusion by which an object seems to the commonsense mind to have inherent qualities, such as sweetness in sugar. Scientific investigation shows that such qualities are not inherent in the article itself, but are our own response to certain featureless events associated with the article. On the other hand, the fact that the events do not possess the qualities we ascribe to them does not mean that they do not exist. Both they and our appreciation of them, though not wholly real, do have a reality, a relative reality; indeed maya is the very stuff of creation, both the weaving and the curtain.

Maya is nearly, but not quite, synonymous with avidya. There is, a subtle and important distinction between the two concepts. When one is thinking of the concept in relation to the impersonal Brahman, the term "maya" is used; but when it is applied to the divine spark within ourselves, the Atman, the term "avidya" is used. In the works of Shankara's followers there have been exceptions to this strict differentiation, but in strict parlance the word "avidya" is reserved for the empirical aspect of the world creative process as seen from the standpoint of the individual soul. In other words, "maya" is used when the energy of the Lord is seen in its creative aspect, "avidya" when we are thinking of its power of veiling; avidya is the cosmic force that in the nature of things veils true knowledge.

Avidya means, etymologically, the antithesis of knowledge — absence of knowledge, but, here, it means far more than mere nescience. It is not a negative concept. All knowledge covering the phenomenal world are embraced by the term Avidya. According to Isa Upanishad, it is through Avidya that one crosses the ford of death, while through Vidya one attains to immortality. Both are of equal importance to the seeker.

First, what is the origin of avidya? It is manifestly an unsound metaphysical position to say that its origin is in Brahman, because Brahman is pure consciousness and absolute knowledge. (We considered this logical difficulty in the last chapter.) It cannot be traced to the individual soul, because individuality itself is a product of avidya. Shankara simply says that it is inexplicable. It is an empirical category, and an attempt to look for its origin in transcendental realms is bound to prove futile. In looking for its origin, we are really asking why the Universe, and ourselves with it, was created. It seems to be a principle of our lives that we cannot know the answer to this question with our finite minds. We often get further towards it by not trying, by resigning ourselves to the will of our Creator, and accepting the framework of pleasure and pain which is allotted to us. Even if we can get no further than to thank him for our "creation, preservation, and all the blessings of this life", it is better than kicking against the walls. But some have discovered a handle at whose mere touch a whole panel of the wall slides back and they are free. Some have denied the existence of the door, and if we are to follow the methods of search of Shankara and the other sages and saints, we shall not know the answer to this question — whether there is a door or not — until we shall have passed through it. We shall not understand avidya until we are beyond its hold, though then there is no "until", because time itself is a product of avidya. Somewhere in every way of life, in every study, there has to be a leap in the dark, an act of faith. Scientists make it every time they assume that their basic assumption of a rational world-model is sound, and that their experiments will therefore repeat.

And how can we feel for the secret spring of the door? It is a help to reflect that our awareness of avidya is in itself a constant reminder that the consciousness is there; avidya is in a sense supported by the pure consciousness, even as the patch of cloud which veils the sun could not be seen without the sun's light. The seat of avidya is the antahkarana, which as we saw in Chapter V is in Shankara's psychology the "inner organ", which in some of its modes of behaviour (vrittis) is the mind (manas), the intellect (buddhi), or the attention (chitta). These entities can be discovered fairly easily in one's own interior by introspection; it does not need any particular insight to find them. They are among the gifts by which avidya can be removed, the thorn which can be used to extract the other thorn of avidya. The intellectual mode alone, be it noted, is not enough: the whole being and thought of the student have to be concentrated on the goal of removing avidya.

It may throw some further light on the concept of maya if we now consider its relationship to the various other entities in Shankara's philosophy. To go back to the beginning, Brahman, the pure spirit of the universe, taken in conjunction with his creative energy — maya — is Ishvara, the personal deity; and, running parallel with that cosmic equation, Atman, the spark divine in the heart of man, taken in conjunction with the power to create appearances — avidya — is the jiva, the individual soul. When avidya is removed, the jiva becomes one with the Atman, the pure consciousness. The desires, yearnings and activities that the jiva exhibits belong in reality not to the jiva but to the avidya. The jiva is associated with the antahkarana, and may be described as the Atman immanent in the antahkarana, the fact of its being immanent being avidya — creation and veiling all in one. From the standpoint of the Atman as a transcendent spirit, the Atman as limited by the antahkarana is called the "Jivasakshin" (S^2 in Chapter V). Putting the matter another way, the antahkarana is an attribute of the jiva and a limitation (upadhi) of the jivasakshin. (The word "upadhi" is not, however, to be understood as a limitation in the ordinary sense. The infinite spirit can never be limited; the limitation is only apparent and not real.)

The nature of the jiva is one of the central points of Shankara's philosophy and he took a good deal of the concept for granted as part of the common fund of religious ideas of his time. This creates a great difficulty for the Western student. The description of the jiva in Sanskrit bristles with technical terms which have not always been used consistently. The terminology does, however, describe aspects of the human soul which can be intuitively perceived by a person who practises the philosophy, though neither these nor any other terms can express the inexpressible core of it. Nor was the terminology invented to solve any philosophical "puzzle"; though Shankara's view of jiva does in fact solve the problem we considered in the last Chapter — namely, how it is possible for God who is perfect to produce from himself an imperfect world, and how he can be said in any sense to be immanent in such a world. Shankara is merely giving orderly philosophical expression to spiritual truths that he himself and the saints and sages before and since his time have come to know in the normal course of their spiritual training.

The essence of the doctrine may be put thus: The jiva has five limiting adjuncts (upadhis) in ascending order of fineness. Starting with the outermost, these may be roughly called (1) the material, (2) the vital, or sheath of the breath, (3) the mental, (4) the intellectual, or the sheath of the buddhi, and (5) the blissful. These divisions are called sheaths (kosas), because they veil the pure consciousness as a sheath veils the sword; the Atman as limited by these upadhis is the jiva. (Neither this nor the more homely onion metaphor that springs to the mind should, of course, be interpreted spatially; though real, the sheaths are no more or no less solid than the Atman or the jiva itself.)

Some men, of the most materialist outlook, identify themselves with the outermost layer of their souls. Those who recognise that living matter is inherently different from dead matter, but do not "reach higher then to compare themselves with the oak or the vine" identify themselves with the vital sheath. Those who have sensibility at the level of feeling—nature's artists — identify themselves with their feelings about the world. These feelings may be very subtly and beautifully expressed, but they are no more than a preparation for direct unitive experience. Those who have learned to grasp abstract ideas (including, alas, most professional philosophers in the West) instinctively identify themselves and the world with what they **think** with their own buddhi. It seems a lofty and pure outlook, and up to a point it is so; but by itself it is not enough. The fifth type is the jiva which identifies itself with the joy and beatitude of the pure spirit right in the core of the onion. To achieve this state, one has to cultivate detachment towards the sheaths, one after another, gradually penetrating deeper.

In transcending these limiting adjuncts, however, the jiva proceeds not by dismissing them as the products of avidya — though that is what they are — but by understanding and developing them in their proper perspective. The material body is not ill-treated; if asceticism is practised, it is to master the body, but not to kill it. It is right to hold wife and little ones dear, though not as an end in itself. If study and learning are given second place, it is not because they are despised but because they are seen to be no more than the label on the bottle. Even the subtle and heavenly joy given by the arts — particularly music — is valued not as an end in itself (even the glorying and rejoicing of a creative artist in his skill should not be so regarded) but as a preparation for the inexplicable joy of union with the divine Atman within.

The jiva strives for liberation through the activity of the antahkarana in its various modes, of which attention or concentration (chitta) is the most important, and reveals the eternal and immutable Atman in a progressively higher glory and power. The mind or intellect is not enough to grasp the whole truth, but when perfect knowledge is gained, the mind itself is transferred as the sky-apperance is transcended when the idea of space is grasped. The jiva can in fact break away from the buddhi only after Reality is directly apprehended; otherwise the buddhi continues to be associated with the jiva from birth to death; and after death it remains latent in the jiva until the jiva is reborn.

The jiva expresses itself empirically towards the outer world by means of the sheaths, which, in considering this aspect of the jiva, may be regrouped into three entities of "bodies": (1) the material body which alone is sloughed off at death, the rest of it being immortal; (2) the subtle body, which includes both the mental and intellectual sheaths, as well as five organs of perception, five of action, and five of "vital forces"; and (3) the causal body. One has to use the material body to experience the subtle world we encounter in dreams, and the causal to experience the causal world we enter in dreamless sleep. In other words, the three bodies correspond to three states of consciousness in which three different worlds are experienced, though each world is supported by the underlying self or Atman. A liberated sage can be conscious of all three worlds — even in his waking state; but the ordinary empirical jiva has three distinct states of consciousness: (1) the waking state, when the Self is associated with the material and subtle bodies together; (2) dreaming, when the Self is associated with the subtle body alone; and (3) deep sleep when the Self merges back into its original state of non-dualised existence and for a time enjoys its original plenitude and beatitude.

In its aspect as underlying the sheaths, or being at the core of the three bodies, the Self or Atman is called the "jivasakshin", which means that it is an unmoved observer of all that the jiva does, enjoys and suffers; it is the "knower of the field"; "it does not eat, for it is the director of both the eater and the eaten". And lest the Atman's alleged direction be misunderstood as a type of activity, Shankara hastens to add that "his mere witnessing is as good as direction, as though he were a king".

Ultimately, the jiva and the Atman, the creature and the creator are one. The jiva is not **part** of the Atman, for the Atman is partless and infinite; it is not a modification of the Atman, because the Atman is immutable; it is not a creation of the Atman, because it shares in the reality of Atman. Some Upanishads speak of jivas as emanations from the Lord, like sparks from fire, but neither this metaphor nor the others used in the sacred books should be worked too hard or taken too far. They are not in the nature of blue prints or drawings of reality — religion without tears. They are more in the nature of crutches, and the healthy soul must in the end learn to do without them.

Two further of these metaphors may, however, help. There is first the one we have used before — the space and the jug. Space does not undergo any modification by being 'confined' to the jug, the limiting walls of which are themselves in space. Yet the space within the jug appears not only as limited but also sullied by such dust and impurities as may be in the jug. When we move the jug, the space in it does not move, and yet it seems to be moving. Even so does the Atman appear to be limited, tainted by sin and propelled by desires to activity when its limiting adjuncts give individuality to it.

The other metaphor is that the jiva is a reflection of the Atman in avidya. When the sun is reflected in water, its brilliance is not in fact diminished, but it appears to be subject to the impurities and movement of the reflector. The sun is not affected; but an undiscriminating person might imagine that it was. In the same way, the characteristics of avidya come to be attributed to the Atman when it is looked upon as the individual soul.

In deep sleep the jiva is said to attain its real nature. Shankara quotes with enthusiasm the Upanishadic saying that the jiva visits the Brahman world day after day without knowing it — meaning in deep sleep. The non-awareness of this visit comes only after waking up from the sleep and reflecting about it in the state of waking consciousness in which avidya is able to operate. Later non-dualists have illustrated this by a story derived from the scriptures. A boy has a bird tied by a long string to his thumb. The bird soars up on its wings, but finding itself unable to break the string — slender as it is — it gives up the struggle and returns to perch on the very thumb to which it is bound. It is fed with sweet and bitter berries until it is sated and takes off again. The bird is the jiva, the air the Brahman world, the thumb the psycho-physical mechanism, the thread the bond of karma and the flight deep sleep.

To recapitulate: The pure Self is Brahman when viewed objectively, and Atman when viewed subjectively. It is God the Father which creates and sustains all things subjectively. Self when associated with maya is Ishvara, the Creator; and when associated with avidya it is the Holy Ghost that inspires the soul and lives at its core. Within the jiva, it is the jivasakshin, the Son ("for we are all sons of God, heirs and joint heirs of the Kingdom of Heaven"). Brahman alone is ultimately Real. When this Reality, this Whole, is realised, everything else — even including Ishvara — is done away.

But in ordinary life, the unliberated soul falsely identifies the Atman, the jivasakshin, with the psycho-physical mechanism, the "sheaths" which make up its earthly vesture. It is our destiny to learn how to look within, to pierce the veil of maya and avidya, and find the Atman in all its glory and power. We have the power to become the sons of God—God himself!

Self In Three States

In reading Western philosophy one is presented almost exclusively with concrete facts manipulated by intellectual processes into an orderly system of knowledge; indeed, to a Western philosopher, the construction of such a system to "explain" the world is the main object of philosophical study. But Vedanta recognises that there are two other states of consciousness, the dream state and the deep-sleep state, and that any philosophical system that lays claim to be comprehensive must take account of all three states. Western philosophy has shown surprisingly little interest in the dream and deep-sleep states, and no attempt is made to fit them into the schemes of the various philosophies. This is remarkable, when one considers that one of the avowed aims of all philosophy — Western and Eastern — is to account for everything, and that sleep is one of the most familiar experiences of life, "the death of each day's life". Moreover, one would have thought that with all their preoccupations with subject and object, philosophers would have shown some curiosity about a state in which the subject seems to disappear. For the extreme subjective idealists, the world is presumably annihilated when the observer falls asleep; but from their own standpoint, the realist schools could hardly deny that the sleeping observer is a part of the objective world, and one would have expected them to try to fit him into their world-pictures. In fact, hardly any of them have seriously tried to do so. In the West, sleep and dreams have appeared as psychophysical phenomena to be tackled from the standpoint of the waking consciousness and intellect, but never as, so to speak, a second and third dimension of the basic consciousness.

How do the three states of consciousness fit into Shankara's philosophy? In his view, the ego is confined to the waking state, and the jiva's contact with the phenomenal world is through the waking state only. The individuality and mental "modes" disappear when the waking state is replaced by either of the other states. This does not mean, however, that the waking consciousness is a product of the phenomenal world. Nobody who took this materialistic view would deny the proposition (which to any but an extreme idealist is practically self-evident) that the world exists before the rise and fall of consciousness in ourselves. For this reason, if for no other, the materialist is forced to regard the subject as one of a number of objects in the world. This is, however, almost a contradiction in terms and lands him back in the old difficulty that the world seems to contain the perceiving mind, while simultaneously the perceiving mind contains the world; for the world is undoubtedly something in the most materialist of minds.

In hunting for a source of reality in the outside world, we are tacitly assuming that our own minds are not real —not in their own right, anyway. Some materials take this to the logical conclusion and hold that mind is a mere "epiphenomenon" — a by-product of the chemical activity of the brain cells, and they are not deterred by the apparently inevitable consequence that this opinion when expressed by them is also an epiphenomenon. But anyone who takes this view has to face the absurd proposition that an unreal mind can know a real universe. All arguments of this kind — even those to disprove the materialist position — can probably be shown to be circular; indeed, the important thing about them is their unsoundness. The only view that makes sense is that somewhere within us there is an observer to whom both subject and object are objects. Our very ideas of life and reality are inherent in ourselves as observers. They reside in our real self. The subject-object relationship is a product of maya, by the process of adhyasa or false attribution. From this standpoint the world is no more or less real than the mind, and in other states of consciousness both are transcended. Both subject and object belong to the realm of things having only a relative reality.

The relevance to our immediate topic — the three states of consciousness — of this digression into epistemology is that the phenomenal world is perceived by us only in one state of consciousness — the waking one. It is not perceived by our whole being. It follows that philosophies based on observation of external facts alone are bound to be incomplete: parts both of the perceiver and of the perceived are missing.

The reality or otherwise of dreams — including daydreams, and illusory beliefs (in unicorns, for example) —is a real philosophical problem and, like telepathy, for instance, presents more difficulty to the deviser of a world scheme of philosophy than the reality or unreality of matter or causation. For sleep and dreams are undoubtedly facts directly experienced in a convincing way that some of the more inaccessible external objects (such as a star or a starch molecule) cannot be. The dreams that occur in sleep are, within their own limits, not less real than the images that present themselves to us in the waking state. They have their own kind of reality and we accept it fully while they last. On the other side, as every physicist knows, the "objective" also seems on close examination to be "such stuff as dreams are made of", and consists largely of empty space occupied by waves of energy. There may be a substratum, but if so, for the physicist it is more in the nature of a flux of energy — something like Bergson's "elan vital" — than the commonsense idea of substance. On the other hand, it is most unlikely to be a mere thought or inconceivable mathematical proposition.

This is not to say that dreams have any special value—on the contrary, they may be about evil things, and daydreams may be harmful fantasies. The point is that they have a relative reality, of the same kind as the reality of perception in the waking state. In the Vedantic view, the subject and object in the dream and their relationship are all created by the Self, the Atman, and illumined, so to speak, by its radiation. Avidya is the source of all perception, sound or illusory. Total fallacies such as a barren woman's son or a square triangle are—to use a somewhat tautological epithet—"defective" avidya, but where there is a conceivable event, even if it is as wildly imaginary as a stone falling upwards, there is "sound" avidya. In the ultimate analysis, such illusory perceptions, whether in dreams, fantasies, or in the waking state, are different only in degree from sound perceptions, in which a table is seen as a table. This may seem a frightening theory at first but a physicist, at any rate, would accept that the perception of a table at a solid object is very much of an approximation. On reflection one realises that the waking consciousness is not so very much more "real" than the dream-in-sleep consciousness. The subject-object relationship, the cause-effect relationship consciousness and memory are present—for what they are worth—in both; and though the present seems very real to the waking consciousness the past is little more than a half-remembered dream.

On the other hand, the dreaming ego and the waking ego are also distinct entities; for quite apart from their different conceptions of time, they move in different ways in different worlds. The waking ego does not dream, nor does the dreaming ego ever wake. When A says he dreamt, he is moving his standpoint from the waking to the dreaming state. He superimposes the dream state on the waking state. This is possible, not because there is any point of identity or continuity between the waking state and the dreaming state, but because there is an underlying consciousness which contains both states.

The sense that the dreamer is himself being perceived in the part he is playing in the dream is further evidence that Atman is the inner light of man. At any rate, it is very difficult to see what other theory could account for self-consciousness in a dream.

The similarity between the dreaming and waking consciousness should not be pressed too far. It is their quality only that is similar; their scope is very different. The dreaming consciousness is limited to the dreamer; it is a private world. The phenomenal world, on the other hand, enters the waking consciousness of all people. In Hindu parlance it is said to be "popular". Had it not been so, as Shankara says, with the attainment of liberation by the first saint the whole world would have been dissolved.

In the third state of consciousness—deep sleep—Shankara, following the Upanishads, held that the jiva merges completely in Brahman. There is no longer differentiated consciousness or individuality, but one undifferentiated consciousness. It is an illustration, in life, of the blessedness of release. (The sense of blessedness one often experiences on waking from deep sleep may be a very simple proof that Shankara's view is true.) In his view, deep sleep is the leveller of all existence—a state that lifts everything and everyone to Brahman day after day. In deep sleep, the consciousness is pure—no avidya, no desire, no action. Particular cognitions cease, since, as the Brihadaranyaka Upanishad asks: "Where all is one, how can one see another?" Referring to a person in deep sleep, the Mandukya Upanishad says: "The Self is the ruler of all; inhabitant of the hearts of all. He is the source of all; creator and dissolver of beings. There is nothing he does not know." This means that the Self, absorbed in Brahman, has all the powers and qualities of Godhead (though, strictly speaking, he has no qualities). Nevertheless, even in deep sleep the Atman is covered, as it were, with a thin veil of maya, which is sufficient to prevent the Atman from simultaneously being conscious of the world. Only to this extent is deep sleep an inferior state to the fourth state of consciousness, called turiya or samadhi, in which the Atman is united with Brahman, at once integrating and transcending all the three states of consciousness.

The three states of consciousness grade into one another but it would be a mistake to suppose that they were adjuncts of each other. They are quite distinct. The dream and the waking states have different and characteristic time series; and time snaps altogether in deep sleep. For it is impossible for anyone to say that at such and such a point of time the waking state ceased and the deep-sleep state began, or that the deep-sleep state ceased and the waking state began. Beginning and ending presuppose the passage of time; and only if the two states had a common time-series would it be possible for them to be continuous. It may be argued that on waking from deep sleep it is common for one to say: "I have slept and I feel refreshed"; and to say, if pressed, "Of course, I remember sleeping". This memory is direct and not inferred as one can test for oneself. On waking from deep sleep the first impression is that one has slept well and not that one feels refreshed or has awakened. If the experience of sleeping had never been presented direct to one's consciousness one would never be sure that it was oneself that had slept. As soon as one begins to think of the facts of awakening or feeling refreshed, however, one's ego is operating in the waking state, in which there is subject-object relationship and consciousness of time. The ego is trying to catch the timeless events of deep sleep and pigeonhole them, which is impossible, because a memory presented to the waking intelect involves a subject-object relation which is absent in the deep-sleep state. What really happens is that the waking ego is dimly aware of the pure consciousness that underlies all three states of consciousness, and to that extent it knows what the deep-sleep state is like; though this vision is seen only dimly through a veil of avidya.

The Upanishadic view of the deep-sleep state has several important implications. The conventional view of cause and effect requires that time should be real, that it should flow on, and that the cause should precede the effect. Therefore, in the deep-sleep state, the cause-and-effect relationship does not exist.

This also throws further doubt on the reality of that relationship in the waking state. In the waking state, the deep-sleep state is seen as a previous state, and the cause of the world in the condition in which it is perceived in the waking state should be its condition in the preceding deep-sleep state. But if there is no time in deep sleep, it is difficult to see how it can be a cause of anything, whether in that state or after it. This view of deep sleep gives a clue to the appearance and disappearance of the phenomenal world and the dream-world, and the operations of adhyasa or illegitimate transference are exposed by the deep sleep state.

All that has been said so far may seem completely unbelievable to the Western student. On reflection, it will not perhaps appear quite so irrational, but, as we have already pointed out, this book is written with the waking intellect and traversed by the waking ego of the reader. We are using our poor blunt thorn of intellect to try to extract the other thorn of avidya. The waking intellect cannot expect to comprehend the three states, and in trying to do so—and still more, to establish their relations to one another—the intellect almost inevitably throws up irrational and inexplicable propositions. The three states are undoubtedly facts of experience, and although in looking at them intellectually we have been compelled to insist on their separateness **at their own level,** they are in fact grounded in the same unity of pure consciousness in which all things are grounded. In order to view the three states as a comprehensible whole, we need the help of intuition—the knowledge that is pure consciousness, self-certifying and incontrovertible. This intuition is called— for the convenience of the waking intellect, so to speak— turiya or samadhi. In this state the jiva is at one with **Brahman** even more completely than in deep sleep. There is not the least veil of maya and the soul is broad awake.

Until this state is achieved, however, the waking intellect will be tormented with the insoluble puzzle—why the pure consciousness should manifest itself in the three different states, and how the unity of the deep-sleep state manifests itself as the diversity of the dream and the waking states. The puzzle is never solved; to the earnest student who attains to a unitary knowledge of Brahman, it does not arise—or if it does, it is irrelevant. This is one of the points at which the fundamental difference between the Indian and the European approach simply has to be accepted. In the Indian view, the sort of knowledge which solves, or rather supersedes, the standard philosophical puzzles, is not attained wholly, or even mainly, by intellectual study. Many intellectuals can conceive the unity of Reality only if the empirical world reveals that unity; the idea that unity and diversity can exist at the same time is inconceivable to them. But when the three states are contemplated and analysed, the real nature of the underlying Atman becomes gradually visible.

To Shankara, the many was an illusion, the one only was real. As he puts it: "The dream state becomes unreal in the waking state, nor does the waking state exist in dream and sleep; both dream and waking state are absent in the deep-sleep state; sleep, too, is absent in waking and in dreams. Because of their mutual contradictions the three states are unreal; but the Self is the Eternal Witness of the three states and is thus beyond them; It is the One which is the nature of pure consciousness".

Ethics

There is no branch of philosophy so extensive, confused, overlapping, and open to misunderstanding as ethics. We have no room here to attempt a survey of ethical problems as formulated in the West; but in order to understand Shankara's attitude and his personal contribution to Hindu ethics we must first make some attempt to grasp the differences in mental and spiritual attitudes between Hindu and European philosophers in their approach to the subject.

One can start anywhere in ethics, but for our purposes a useful point of departure may be the time-honoured argument advanced by Glaucon in Plato's Republic. Put very briefly, he contended that man is a selfish and savage animal, and in the state of nature which existed before society came into being each man was at active enmity with any other who came within his reach. But when human beings came to live in society, they found that open and unbridled enmity did not pay, and so each individual entered into a contract to restrain his fellow-citizens and himself from the worst sorts of social misconduct. Within defined limits, honesty became the best policy. And thus we have our ideas of good behaviour and a well-regulated society. Plato portrays Socrates as refuting these arguments, producing in the process a complete sketch of a "just" society. With the details of this society we are not concerned here; what is significant for our purpose is that in many pages of complex syllogistic reasoning nobody pauses to question whether man ever existed in a state of nature of the sort supposed, or why, if everybody hated everybody else so much, they ever came together in societies at all. Plato was apparently happy to labour at a proposition as unreal as Shankara's "barren woman's son". Some European philosophers—notably Kant—have, it is true, made valiant attempts to produce systems that are not merely intellectually and verbally watertight but are related to the problems of men and women in society as it really exists; but most of them have been bedevilled by the tacit assumption that ratiocination is a good thing in itself, and they have usually shown the same lack of critical curiosity as Plato about the basic material of their study. Moreover, most of them have not been troubled by the contradictory conclusions of their different systems; the more cynical have admitted that if they were to agree there would be nothing more to talk, write and lecture about.

Now Hindu philosophy has little in common with this outlook. It is concerned with practical moral problems, and not with ethical theories; with the tacit assumptions on which people really act, and not with the reasons they produce for their actions. For the problems of ethics are real, and, paradoxically, the more urgent they are, the more difficult they are to reduce to intellectual terms.

The difficulties of formulation are so great that some philosophers have questioned whether it is possible to talk about ethics at all. May not our ideas about right and wrong be a private illusion? Perhaps there is nothing right or wrong but thinking makes it so. This is an attitude which is practically impossible either to prove or disprove, and at some point in trying to do so one is practically certain to assume the truth or falsehood of the proposition itself. One can only say that nobody seems to regulate his life on this principle. If somebody who has been arguing that right is a matter of personal opinion is faced with an unlawful demand for money, he will rush to the Courts for redress with emotional conviction!

Some philosophers do not go as far as this ethical "nihilism", but hold the theory of ethical "silence": namely that a person can receive valid moral ideas into his own mind but cannot communicate them to others. Ethical ideas have an ultimate quality which is by its very nature incommunicable to others—like the idea of redness. One can establish by a consensus of opinion that a certain article is red, but this amounts to no more than an agreement to give a certain name to a certain colour; the actual experience of redness is not communicated from one to another.

Hindu ethics does not accept either of the foregoing propositions. It holds that moral ideas have a real existence, and that they can be and are communicated to others. We are intuitively aware of our portion of the divine Self, and we are aware of the Self in others. One's own experience of goodness must therefore be recognisably the same as that of another—that is if our intuition has become perfect.

But even if this is conceded, most European philosophers would hasten to point out that ideas of right and wrong seem to vary from place to place and from one person to another, and would be inclined to inquire if there is **any** absolute standard. Can any Englishman ever come to the same conclusion as a Hindu, or a Buddhist, or a Russian? The Hindu answer is that good and evil have only a relative reality. They exist in the material world and share in its unreality, and the inconsistencies between the different schools of philosophy arise mainly because they are all looking around for a standard in the material world. For an Englishman, murder of an Englishman is a crime, but for much of this century murder of a German, another human being though with a different passport, has been a virtue. "I am firm, thou art obstinate, he is pig-headed." It is only when we come to know the divine Brahman in ourselves and recognise it in others in spite of external differences that the possibility of perceiving one absolute standard arises. It is some practical confirmation of this in that the words and deeds of the saints, sages and mystics, both Western and Eastern, conform very closely to a pattern—a perennial philosophy, to use Aldous Huxley's phrase.

In any event, there is no hope of arriving at moral principles that are not downright absurd unless one starts from some metaphysical conception of the world—some assumption as to what the world is and what each one of us as an individual is in it for. As Dr. Albert Schweitzer says: "Ethics has no significance in a world devoid of meaning. A man's ethical life in such a world must be limited to keeping himself pure from it". (Astonishingly, Dr. Schweitzer then drew the conclusion that the

Hindus regarded the world as a meaningless game; but that is another matter, and is a standing warning as to the difficulty of writing **about** ethics. In his own life, Dr. Schweitzer has put into effect the precepts of Hindu ethics!)

There is another important class of ethical theory to which Hindu ethics does **not** belong: the "utilitarian", namely, that the criterion of actions is whether their results are good or bad. A famous example is that an action should result in "the greatest good of the greatest number". In the first place, this approach leaves for discussion the all-important question as to what is to be regarded as a "good" result. Most utilitarians hold in one form or another that "good" consists in the pursuit of happiness. J. S. Mill says outright: "Pleasure and freedom from pain are the only things desirable as ends." But he saw that this low view of "good" as physical pleasure would lead to his morality being regarded as "immoral", and he therefore introduced the concept of an additional type of pleasure of a higher or more subtle order—by which he almost certainly meant the pleasure of philosophising! But even if one is clear about the nature of the good one is aiming at, there is still the objection that one cannot be sure that one will in fact attain the good; nobody can forecast the results of actions with any certainly. Suppose one rescues a man from drowning and he then straightaway goes home and murders his wife and children? Would it not have been "better" to let him drown?

More important for our purpose than "official" philosophical theories, however, are the tacit assumptions of a generally utilitarian kind held by large numbers of average people in this work-a-day world. For example, it is "good" if two blades of grass grow where one grew before, or the output of refrigerators goes up by twenty per cent. A sweet pea four times as big as the old Victorian one — even if it has no scent — is obviously four times as good and more than four times as likely to win a prize in the flower show. More subtly, a man is a "better" man if he can do differential equations or to speak with an Oxford or some other special accent.

A.S.—4

These tacit assumptions carry with them the further assumptions that anything good must produce results in the material world — and that provided the results make a loud noise it does not matter much what kind of results they are. One must march with a powerful, and preferably a winning, side. Ambition becomes one of the greatest virtues, because it is the source of the most striking results. The man who on grounds of principle votes for a small minority party is accused, with significant and quite disproportionate heat, of "throwing away his vote". He is committing the sin not only of not being on the winning side, but of failing to be.

In contrast of these views, Hindu ethics hold (1) that the value of an action resides ultimately in its effect on the doer; and (2) that the pursuit of pleasure in any form, however subtle, as an end in itself is a delusion.

In the language of Western ethics, Hindu ethics is frankly "intuitionist". We know in our hearts that certain types of behaviour are intrinsically good and others bad, regardless of their result. This does not mean, as many suppose, that the Hindu view is purely "subjective"; namely, that every man should follow his own idea of the good, and be indifferent to what happens to others. The distinction between the subjective and the objective is in the last analysis unreal, and it follows that Hindu ethics will seem, when it is being described, to have both subjective and objective aspects, which are ultimately perceived to be the same. The essence of virtuous behaviour in the eyes of the Hindu is that it is both a precondition to liberation and an active help towards it. The ordinary man owes his sense of virtue to the Atman within him, but owing to avidya he starts off with a most imperfect knowledge; his vision of the truth is mixed with error, and through that ignorance he commits faults. To purify his actions he needs more knowledge of the Atman, and to know the Atman he must purify his actions. This would be a vicious and unbreakable circle but that God has implanted in every man a desire to come to him, which will sooner or later bring about his liberation, even if at present he seems to be always running off after every pleasurable red-herring. Even the yearning for ease and pleasure is itself a fractional manifestation of the all-pervading desire for the supreme and absolute beatitude of Brahman. All we do—in work, play, love-making, family life, in every phase of our activity—springs from a yearning for the supreme happiness. Fraud, rape and murder, too, are committed by those who seek happiness; but, blinded by avidya, they seek it by the wrong path. The point is that, as Shankara says, everyone does strive for happiness and not for misery; it is the pursuit of earthly happiness as an end in itself that is the mistake.

How does the individual come into the right path? In Shankara's opinion, in addition to practising virtue, he must take the advice of a teacher, perform rituals, and read the scriptures. If he does not want to do any of these things, he can make no progress for the moment and the day of his liberation is not yet. But sooner or later he will take the decisive steps; liberation is his destiny, though the finding of it is an act of his own free-will.

We must now make a short digression into the vexed question of free-will and determinism. A great many arguments have been advanced on both sides of this matter, but no conclusive solution on the level of reasoning has been found, or is likely to be. Before trying to present the Hindu view, there are some preliminary observations we should offer:

(1) The whole validity of ethics and even the meaning of ethical judgments would vanish if there were not some freedom to choose different paths, both of thought and of conduct. This proposition has, it is true, been denied by some Western philosophers, particularly scientific materialists. On their view, human society is subject to the same laws of cause and effect as the rest of the living world. Good conduct is simply successful adaptation to the norm of society, and even the power to adapt is determined by the natural heritage and upbringing of the individual. The only successful departures tolerated are those which increase the efficiency of the social group.

In the most extreme forms of this doctrine it is held that mental events are unreal — mere by-products of the electrical operations in the brain which go on automatically as part of our existence. Free will is a mental state and nothing more. It is an inescapable consequence of this view that the view itself is a pre-determined reaction on the part of those who hold it, and it is extraordinary that such people should hold any ethical views at all. It does not follow that determinism is necessarily wrong, but it seems to deprive itself of any **validity.**

(2) In real life, everybody behaves as if he thought his will was free, and people can visibly be seen to choose less pleasant courses — if only to gain some greater but more remote pleasure.

The point at which the fallacy enters is that the scientist — whether physicist, biologist or psychologist — assumes that his picture of the world — a world composed of carefully-defined entities such as "atoms" "genes", "instincts", etc., abstracted from the material world — is all that there is in the universe. Religion is "nothing but" a psychological state. Love is "nothing but" sex. But scientific formulations are not a complete account of the world, even on their own level. To see a table as a mass of vibrating moles separated by substantial amounts of empty space does not describe it completely, even to a physicist, who may for example be studying it simply to measure its thermal conductivity. And when one comes to a human being with a body, mind and spirit strangely interacting, the dangers of abstraction become greater still. It is quite true that sexual behaviour follows certain laws; but it is not true to say that "therefore" love is nothing but sex. It is in the "nothing but" that the fallacy enters.

Now, the Hindus have never worried about the mind v. body problem to the extent that Western, and particularly English philosophers have done. The various aspects of man and his surroundings have always seemed to the Hindus to be part of a world that is rational on all its levels. There is no erratic or capricious heavenly power, like the Greek gods, who sport with man and bring him to inevitable disaster. Nor is there a once-for-all life for the soul, ending in everlasting bliss for the few and flaming perdition for the many. On the other hand, Hindu philosophy does not offer any hope that in return for faith our past wrong-doing can be washed away by the vicarious suffering of a manifestation of God. There can be no scapegoat. Every man must bear his own burden.

The Hindu view is based on the concept of "karma", which means both (1) cause and effect, and (2) ritual. It is also the nearest thing to sin in the Hindu view of life. The law of karma is thus set out in an Upanishad: "As is his desire, so is his purpose; as is his purpose, so is his deed; as is his deed, so does he reap". The suffering of the present is the inevitable consequence of the errors of the past, possibly of errors in a past existence, for the constant returning of the soul to earth until it is finally liberated is fundamental to the Hindu scheme of things. This may seem a deterring thought, but on the other hand, the present is an endless succession of opportunities to achieve a salvation that is promised as an ultimate certainty. At every second of his life, a man stands at the fork in the road between right and wrong; between the path which leads to liberation and the path away from it. The path is determined, but the immediate future is free.

It would seem to follow logically from the concept of karma that if evil deeds bear evil fruit, good deeds bear good fruit, and if one can fill one's life with deeds sanctified by the scriptures, one should achieve salvation — at any rate, in the course of many incarnations. These ritualistic practices should create, as it were, beneficent karma. Shankara did not altogether accept this view. For him an element of **knowledge** of the Atman within was essential to salvation. He did not, however, decry the utility of actions prescribed by the scriptures. If such actions are performed without forgetting that they are aids to liberation, but no more, they will not cling to the soul, either for good or ill; for the wheel of cause and effect is, as it were, a kind of "original sin" inherent in the very fabric of our existence, and even good actions are in the last analysis a hindrance to liberation. It follows that the ultimate aim is to act so that **nothing** clings. A little reflection will show that when that state is reached, the problem of fate and free-will is not solved; but it is transcended.

We can now return to considering the main tenets of Hindu philosophy, which, as we have seen, has both subjective and objective aspects. The subjective aspect rests on two main foundations — asceticism (sannyasa) and harmlessness (ahimsa). Hindu asceticism does not mean the hair-shirt approach, as the Western reader may jump to conclude. The Bhagavad Gita calls people fools who torture their bodily organs, and extols the man who is temperate in his food and recreation, temperate in his exertion at work, temperate in sleep and waking. None of the great Indian philosophers has ever recommended self-immolation, flagellation or other masochistic practices. Shankara was no exception, and although he appreciated the value of the yogic disciplines, he condemned some of the more severe types of physical yoga. Nor is a monastic life essential to the practice of sannyasa. Some devotees do retire from the world for a time, but many can be found actively and vigorously carrying on the world's work.

The basic ideas of Hindu asceticism are: (1) It does not mistake the pleasant for the good ("He who chooses the pleasant fails of his aim.... The mind of the wise man draws him to the good, the flesh of the fool drives him to the pleasant"), (2) The stress is on self-denial. Good actions are valued in proportion to one's reluctance to do them — not, however, in proportion to any intrinsic disagreeableness they may have. This attitude is a logical consequence of the metaphysical position outlined in this study. The conquest of moral reluctance is a conquest of the ego, the removal of one more layer of avidya. The Bhagavad Gita says: "Let a man lift himself up by himself; let him not lower himself; for the Self alone is the friend of the Self. Self alone is the enemy of the Self. To him who has conquered himself by his Self, his very Self is like an external enemy". The general attitude of the Hindu towards bodily desires is shown by the celebrated illustration from the katha Upanishad, in which the body is compared to a chariot, the intellect or discriminating faculty to the charioteer, the mind to the reins, the senses to the horses, the sense-objects to the roads, and the soul to the driver of the chariot. Sannyasa is indeed nothing more than a recognition of the fact that control of the emotions and desires is an aid to spiritual progress. The aim is not the renunciation of worldly objects as such, but of the false values attached to the objects.

It is a great danger of all asceticism that there are true and false kinds that look very much alike. Sannyasa is not to be practised by anybody and every body; and it has to be practised according to rules discovered and handed down by tradition. Premature attempts to become an ascetic, or attempts to do so if it is not at this stage the right thing to do, are all comdemned unequivocally by Shankara. The true renunciation grows and ripens from within in the course of the soul's evolution. Such renunciation is not easy, nor is it an emotional thing. As Stevenson said, "to renounce without bitterness is a task to engage all a man's strength"; but success brings the joy of him who "having nothing yet hath all".

The other great virtue in the Hindu ethical pattern is harmlessness — ahimsa. There is some variation of emphasis between the different schools of Indian philosophy on other topics, but all of them put this virtue very high. It does not mean mere avoidance of hurting people — indeed, a man's social duty may sometimes force him to hurt others — but an active, positive, loving toleration of others, even when we think their ideas are false or their actions evil. We are not to love our enemies so as to bring coals of fire on their heads, but because it is our own duty and part of our own way to liberation.

Although in the last analysis all virtue is valued as an aid to the liberation of the doer, Hindu ethics has also its objective aspect. Certain types of action are recognised as being inherently right in the phenomenal world. Right action has still only a relative reality, but it has greater reality than wrong action, for right action leads to that most real of all facts, the liberation of a human soul, but wrong action is a discouraging incident on the way.

Moreover, rightness is perceived by the consensus of opinion of those who have made some headway — even if only a little — towards liberation. This consensus admittedly does not prove anything. The mystics may **all** have been wrong, and it must fairly be admitted that the circle can only be broken by acts of "faith" — to put no higher a meaning on that word than a willingness to experiment. In the material world we see through a glass, darkly, and this results in differences of opinion on the rightness of particular actions in particular places. But the saints have shown again and again by what they have said and written, and still more by their lives, that the mirror reflects a single pure thing, and that if the mirror could become perfect, the variations in the vision would vanish away.

The basis of objective Hindu morality is the doctrine of dharma, which may be freely translated as "righteousness" or "duty". Dharma is determined to a considerable extent by a man's position in society. In ancient India, this meant his caste. This is not the place for a discussion of this question, which has aroused strong prejudices and predilections. The points to note here are: (1) caste system of ancient India was much more live and positive, and also more flexible, than the system found in modern times. (2) Whatever terms may be used, there is — for good or ill, and usually for both — a class structure in practically all societies; every man finds himself with a place to fill and a part to play in life. Sometimes he plays different parts at once — each of which brings him in contact with different ones of his fellows. He may be a stockbroker's clerk during the day, a sidesman at the Church on Sundays, and on Saturday mornings a golfer bent on reducing his handicap. But to every part attach natural duties, and it is these duties — not those of some other man in some other part — that each man must try to accomplish. A classical example, with a modern application, is in the Bhagavad Gita itself. At the point where the book opens, Arjuna, the prince, born in the warrior caste and leader of one of the opposing factions on the battlefield, is appalled at the thought that on the morrow's battle he will inevitably have to

kill his own kindred. But God, disguised as his charioteer, explains that there is no escape from his duty.
Another man might abstain or be a pacifist, but to Arjuna
himself it was not permitted.

In addition to his duties in society, man has certain
common duties which are the basis of his moral life in
the material world. Different philosophers put different
virtues at the top, but the lists show a revealing similarity. A typical example is: steadfastness, forgiveness,
avoidance of theft, control of the senses, wisdom, learning, truthfulness, and absence of anger. Another list;
charity, helping the distressed, social service; truthfulness, helpful speech, gentleness of speech; tenderness,
detachment, reverence. Another: non-injury (ahimsa),
truthfulness, abstention from theft, continence, detachment. Of course, many of these virtues manifestly begin
with attitudes in the individual himself and would have
a good effect on him whatever their outward results, and
they are to that extent subjective; the objective and the
subjective can never be entirely isolated.

There are some interesting omissions from these lists.
The Englishman's invariable favourite — courage —
does not appear; nor does the socially-minded ancient
Greek's "justice". It is not that the Hindus would not
regard these as virtues, but that they are secondary virtues. Courage is useless unless there is something worth
while to be brave about; the Hindu rejects the idea that
if only you get your name in the headlines it does not
matter how you do it. Justice in the Greek sense is also
secondary, because if individuals practise the virtues
listed, and in particular ahimsa, "justice" would automatically appear.

The average Westerner is most reluctant to accept this
last fact. The difference between his view and the Hindu
view is subtle but deep-seated, and those who wish to
get to the bottom of it will need to ponder it deeply, and
not merely to read or argue about it. It may be a useful exercise, however, to imagine oneself unjustly accused of fraud, and having as the sole witness to the truth
either (1) a well-meaning, worldly-wise humanist, or (2)
a "religious fanatic" who for the purely selfish reason of

desiring his own salvation will tell the truth regardless of the consequences to himself or anybody else. In the first case, would not one be anxiously assessing whether one's witness would "have his family to consider" or "not want to get mixed up in it", and might seek to avoid giving offense by making vague and careful glosses on the facts? But with the second witness, one would, if innocent, have nothing to fear. The practical measure of A's morality is the confidence it evokes in B. Whatever he may say about A's selfishness, B will not in real life be influenced out of relying on A by the argument that A is merely using him as a means to his own spiritual ends.

Except where we have explicitly referred to Shankara's own views, most of what has been said so far applies to practically all Hindu and Buddhist philosophy. We can now look at Shankara's individual contribution. It is dominated by his strictly non-dualist metaphysics, and by his aim at the highest unity of man with God. His ethics is therefore strictly subjective. Ethical disciplines are valued as a prerequisite for contemplation. On the other hand, quietism and retirement from the world are not recommended — at any rate for the beginner. He should carry out all the duties of life, but without desire for results or earthly rewards. These practices do not directly produce liberation; but they generate in the seeker's mind the desire for knowledge, and give him the increased insight necessary to obtain it and thus begin to break the vicious circle. The greater insight leads to better acts, to greater discipline, and so to greater insight again. But it is one of Shankara's main tenets that only knowledge can ultimately bring liberation.

In Shankara's view, the origin of good and evil as contrasted qualities resides in the objective aspect of avidya, i.e., in maya, which from this point of view is rightly translated as "illusion". The main illusion is that one's environment, including other jivas, is separate from oneself. Marcus Aurelius (whose reflections are shot through with the same spirit as Hindu ethics) sets this out very well: "Begin in the morning by saying to thyself, I shall meet with the busybody, the ungrateful, arrogant, deceitful, envious, unsocial. All these things happen to them by reason of their ignorance of what is good and evil. But I who have seen the nature of the good ... can neither be injured by any of them ... nor can I be angry with my kinsman nor hate him".

The delusion that we are separate from others is the source of suffering. The effect of maya is felt in its full bitterness when the individual soul identifies himself with his body, mind, and senses — in short, with his ego. For his ego is the one thing that distinguishes him from others, and conflict is inevitable. He that saveth his life shall lose it, and he that loseth his life for the sake of the deity within, shall find it. The solution to the paradox comes when one perceives that the distinction between subject and object is itself a product of maya, and that it is of no consequence whether moral conduct is aimed at one's own salvation or the salvation of others. The two are so closely bound up that the one implies the other. Shankara would not cling to "nice" people whom he liked while avoiding "unpleasant" people whom he disliked. Nor is it a question of "turning the other cheek"; the aim is to be exactly the same towards the helpful as towards the difficult or dangerous, and to take no notice of the results of such impartiality. It has been aptly said that the aim in conversation is to be able to talk well when one does not want to talk at all, and to be silent when one feels an over-mastering desire to talk. This would be fully accepted by Shankara. Indifference is, again paradoxically, as much to be avoided as hatred.

The non-dualist's love extends equally to animals and other living things. It also extends, again paradoxically, to his own body: when he is not identified with it, he can love it as he can the body of another, or an animal or plant. In this state, the student usually enjoys exceptionally good health and energy; but it is contingent on his remaining detached from his body, conscious always that his true Self is within and sees the body as an object. In other words, the non-dualist practises both self-denial and self-affirmation, but "self" is used in two different senses; it is the egotistical self that is denied, the Eternal Self affirmed.

With this substratum to his teaching, it follows that Shankara held no political views in the modern sense. Above all, he did not share any of the tacit political assumptions that underlie the life of most people in the modern world. For those who now almost instinctively look for "good" in "social welfare" it is well to remember that much of their present mental climate derives from the miseries of the Industrial Revolution and of the mass unemployment which survived into the lifetime of the older generation of Europeans. Ancient India was for long periods prosperous and at peace, and the care of the unfortunate was provided for by the doctrine of dharma. In this way it was recognized that the individual owed part of his significance to the social group in which he lived, and conversely that what he thought and did was of significance to the group. But the social group was seen as at most a means to a spiritual end, a place in which the individual sought his salvation; whereas in the West the group has come to be regarded as an end in itself, to which one should dedicate oneself. Unfortunately, there are over eighty such groups — counting sovereign states alone. It is simple logic that they cannot all be the best in the world; they cannot all be God; and it is not surprising that the fruit of this polytheism should be so discouraging. In Germany after the last war it was common for perfectly healthy people to fall down dead — simply because the defeat of the regime to which they had attached their loyalty had taken away their whole reason for living. Again, the atomic bombing of Japan has been defended on the ground that it saved Allied lives. This proposition was obviously only valid if the Allied lives were inherently more valuable than Japanese lives. This was believed at the time because Japan was a hostile deity, and people with Japanese passports inherently wicked. Now that the Japanese are back into some sort of favour, the inherent wickedness is being transferred to people in other lands with other ideas of life and society.

Even in the democratic countries, the genuine objector to his country's policies is regarded as immoral, a traitor — whatever the grounds of his objection. The difference between the democracies and the totalitarian states is not in the valuation of objectors, but in the vigour with which they are penalised. Where there is a sense of security and a tradition of moderation built up in a secure past — as in England — objectors are more or less unmolested; but where the majority feel themselves threatened, then the minority must beware.

Again it is a tacit assumption, common in both the "free world" and the Communist countries, that anything which increases material prosperity is bound to be "good", and everybody is surprised and distressed that the wonderful developments of science, engineering and medicine have not produced more net benefit. The British Welfare State — a thing which, if it were their personal responsibility, all men when having an intuition of truth would support — has not been an unmixed blessing, even on its own level. A country doctor remarked ruefully that before the war his patients had tuberculosis and rickets, and after the war they had gastric ulcers and neuroses. The Hindu would not be surprised at this. In his view, the relative world is supported by the twin pillars of good-evil, pain-pleasure, and other "pairs of opposites". The sum total of happiness does not change. It simply moves from one place to another. The element of imperfection — of original sin, if one likes — is inherent in the phenomenal world as a whole, but it is the end of the individual to strive for that which is perfect. History undoubtedly does show progress in toleration and in welfare in some directions; but it is difficult in the face of thousand-bomber and atomic air-raids and concentration camps to argue that the twentieth century is really any better for the average citizen to live in than the seventeenth or the thirteenth.

The fact is that the actions of social groups do not have more significance as such; they are part of the phenomenal world and follow the laws of cause and effect that operate in that world. Any moral significance they may possess resides in the individual's approval or condemnation of them. While he is still blinded by avidya, he will attribute good and evil to political acts, but as the follower of Shankara begins to see more clearly, he will stop taking sides and his compassion will extend to all men of all nations and kindreds and peoples and tongues — and of all colours, both of skin and of politics. This does not mean that the follower of Shankara should not play his part, but it does mean that he should not be attached to results on the political and social level. He will perform the civic duties that fall to him wherever he may be situated, and he will support all things which would be good if he were personally responsible for them; but he will not pursue any political theory or support any political party for its own sake. If he does his duty to his country, it is because it is dharma for him, not because his country has necessarily deserved it. He goes on his way quietly, not rushing on martyrdom in a defiant way, but always prepared to lay down his life rather than depart from the way that leads to liberation. Radhakrishnan sums up Shankara's view on this subject in the words: "The perfect man lives and dies, not for himself, but for mankind. It is, however, true that Shankara asks us to be in the world but not of it, even as a drop of water is on the lotus without getting mixed up with it. The part of wisdom is to dream with our eyes open, to be detached from the world without any hostility to it."

It is a curious implication of Shankara's metaphysical position that action performed by a merely "moral" man cannot by itself achieve the highest good, though the same action performed by a liberated man will do so. This may seem superstitious, but a little reflection will show that it is what one should expect. A man who does charitable work to compensate for his own neuroses may seem to be doing good, and in individual cases the result may be achieved. He may even on occasion be the means of grace to others. But all the while he is entangled in the struggle between good and evil and is attached to the results of his actions, one cannot rely on him. As Nikhilananda says in an introduction to some of the Upanishads: "All actions ordinarily bind their doers by creating attachment to the result. It is not action but the desire for the result that brings suffering. Therefore the doer is asked to relinquish all attachment to the re-

sult. Though his body and senses perform action, his
mind must remain unruffled in success and failure.
Hinduism advocates renunciation in action, not renunciation of action. A duty must be done, regardless of its
result, because it ought to be done."

The liberated or illumined person is called a jivanmukta, or free soul. Shankara achieved this state, and
although such souls are rare, they do exist even in this
imperfect world. The injunction "Be ye perfect, even as
your Father in Heaven is perfect" is meant to be taken
literally, and not merely as a pious statement of an unattainable object. As it says in the Upanishad, a jivanmukta becomes, "Free from evil, free from taint, free
from doubts, and a knower of Brahman".

We have described above some of the qualities displayed by the liberated person, and one might say that
he approximated to the idea of sainthood in the West.
This would be true, but only up to a point. The liberated person does not so much become wholly good; he
transcends good and evil. He is not under any moral
compulsion. Ethical values have ceased to apply to him.
He performs good actions — Shankara himself was one
of the most untiring social workers of his time — but
he does so as an apple-tree bears apples, because it is
his nature. He sees the indwelling God in all men, and
his services to them are a kind of worship. Every man
is his neighbour. It is no matter that some recipients of
his love may be unworthy or ungrateful, they will come
to love in the same way as he does, when their liberation
is at hand; if not in this incarnation, then in another.

Nor is there any impurity in the world to one who has
risen above impurity. Other people and all the world
around him are seen to be an illusion, it is true, but he
calls it an illusion on his knees, for its author is no less
than Brahman.

But perhaps we should allow Shankara himself to have
the last word: "The great souls," he says, "calm and
tranquil, live, regenerating the world like the spring; and
themselves having crossed the dreadful ocean of embodied existence and death, help those who struggle for the
same end, without the least trace of personal motives."

Summum Bonum

At the beginning of Chapter III we set out to look at Shankara's philosophy from a series of standpoints in turn. The student whose patience has endured thus far may well expect a neat and succinct summing up; but he must be disappointed. Life cannot be reduced to a few simple intellectual formulations. On the other hand, in the practice of the best men, there is, paradoxically, an extreme simplicity. Just as for the 14th. century English mystic there was the "little word love" and the "little word God", so far the follower of Shankara the highest good of man's existence is nothing more or less than the realisation of identity with Brahman. Only the sense of "I"-ness identified with the body, and "mine"-ness identified with its surroundings, stand between man and the happiness of that realisation.

As Swami Vivekananda says: "When you think you are a body, you are apart from the universe; when you think you are a soul, you are a spark from the Eternal Fire; when you think you are the Atman, you are All". Shankara insists upon the Upanishadic statement: "All would forsake him who recognizes anything as existing elsewhere than in the Self". Man can never be satisfied with material possessions; the more he gets, the more he yearns for. The horizon of happiness recedes ever further. But as it does so it points the discerning to a state of perfect and infinite bliss. The craving is, after all, the dimly-felt Brahman within. Ultimately it will not be in vain, and Brahman-realisation will give the permanent and unalloyed joy that the soul thirsts for.

Brahman can be realised only through perfect knowledge or wisdom. The study of the Vedas and the performance of acts prescribed in them, such as fasting, prayer and ascetic practices, are valuable only in so far as they lead to that knowledge. Duties towards family, friends and society, rightly and unselfishly performed, also help to refine the mind. These should not, however, be regarded as ends in themselves but only as · means to the supreme end. The blind observance of secular laws, or even scriptural injunctions, cannot lead to salvation, though they may lead to increasing prosperity in this world, and, on Shankara's world-view, in the next.

Shankara distinguishes four steps of spiritual progress. The lowest is that occupied by those guided by instincts and impulses, who do not subject themselves either to the scriptural disciplines of the Vedas or to any higher law. These beings, after death, are re-born as flies, gnats or some such lower organisms. Next come those who, though observing the Vedic rules to the letter, acquire neither wisdom nor piety. When these die they are sent to the lunar regions to enjoy there the fruits of their labours performed on earth, and, after exhausting all the rewards for the good deeds, are re-born. The next higher stage comprises those who, in addition to performing the duties prescribed in the scriptures and avoiding those that are taboo, are devoted to the worship of what a Christian would call a personal god — or rather gods, for there are several, the highest of whom is Hiranyagarbha, or Ishvara. In so far as he has a rational understanding of the significance of these gods and worships them, or the highest God, as different from himself, he can attain after death the Kingdom of God, or Brahmaloka. Such souls live with the gods in Brahmaloka at the feet of the highest God until in the end he is merged with Brahman at the end of a cycle, when all things are absorbed back into the spirit that created them. This process is a liberation for the soul, and is not so far distant as might appear from the Christian view, though any parallelism between the lower gods and the saints (including Jesus as a saint for this purpose); between Ishvara and God the Father; and between Brahman and the Holy Ghost should not be pressed too far—if only because the saints are also identified with Brahman. On the other hand, in the Hindu system Jesus would not occupy the unique status of Very God of Very God and the sole way of approach to the Father. This does not mean that Hindu thought in its highest expression is polytheistic; the concept of

the all-pervading Brahman infuses a little of the Godhead into each mortal man, and is always the same everywhere, though the paths to the realisation of Brahman
may be many. There are many paths up the hill of holiness, but there is only one summit.

The fourth and the highest state of souls is the state
of those who through the highest or absolute knowledge
realise their complete identity with Brahman. At this
level, there is not even knowledge of Brahman; the soul
has become absolute knowledge and is Brahman. All the
knowledge which was acquired in the course of striving
for this end, and which finally brought it about, falls off
like an arrow after it has hit the target. In another metaphor, absolute knowledge destroys all ignorance and is
itself destroyed as a flame burns a heap of grass and then
extinguishes itself.

In this state, which is the same as the fourth state of
consciousness or turiya, there is a merging in it of the
three other lower states — waking, dreaming and deep
sleep. This fourth state is the highest or real consciousness, and is spotlessly pure. It includes the other three
states and transcends them. It is immediate experience,
and the world is, so to speak, sunk in it. It is above all
relatedness and is one with the absolute, which includes
all related things. There is no activity then, either of
thought or of heart; for all activity is a product of the
illusory consciousness of one's own ego as a thing separate from the world. There is no duality in the turiya
state; everything has become merged in the Self.

This state of release is not capable of production
like a jug from clay; nor is it brought about through
mortification, like curds from milk; nor is it capable of
being reached, like a home by a traveller; nor is it to be
attained through mere internal purification, like the clean-
ing of a soiled mirror. It is an indefinable, inexpressible intuition that one is Brahman. It is not an acquired state like
paradise, nor does it reside in being in the same world
as Brahman; for these being attained results, admit of
degrees of excellence rising pari passu with the quality
of devotion. In another metaphor, the soul is not lost
like an individual in a crowd, but is absorbed as a drop

of rain water in the sea, after which the drop assumes the vastness and might of the sea wholly and completely. This state cannot be equated with anything else, because it includes everything else and leaves nothing outside itself.

To the Western mind, which is conditioned to think in terms of a single earthly life for each soul, and a hereafter dependent not so much on spiritual achievement as on redemption by God himself, Shankara will seem to set the sights impossibly high. In one life, with all our past sin, only a miracle of redemption can save us. To Shankara, however, it was axiomatic that the soul could return again and again to the earth; indeed, it does so only too easily; salvation, the **summum bonum,** resides in escaping from the round of births into union with God. That all are destined ultimately to attain this liberation is a simple axiom for Shankara. This does not mean that Shankara hated this life or despised it; his aim is to make us **transcend** our earthly life. Whether one achieves liberation depends to some extent on past karma, but with sufficient effort one may accomplish this state in this very life. When one has thus become a liberated sage, a jivanmukta, no fresh karma, can accrue, and the effects of past actions will be obliterated. The karma actually in process of formation at the time of liberation will have to be accepted, but it cannot slam the door of realisation in one's face, for already it begins to belong to a past life that is unreal.

Strictly speaking, from the point of view of ultimate reality, even liberation is illusory. Shankara says: "If there is no bondage in our origin and dissolution, neither is there liberation: just as there is neither night nor day in the sun: the appearance of it is due to a limitation in our vision". Bondage and liberation are **in** the world but they do not lie at the root of the world; they are not in Brahman. But from our own standpoint in the world; where our vision is veiled by avidya, we have to strive to find the real; and we are often as foolish in our search as the girl who is wearing an ornament on her neck but forgets where it is and looks for it high and low.

After the experience of liberation, the jivanmukta continues to live in this world for some time until the karma with which he was caught at the time of liberation has exhausted itself. Like the potter's wheel that continues to revolve for a few turns after the vessel is finished, his life continues by its own momentum. Absolute and final release comes only with death. The liberated soul, on being separated from the body, merges itself in Brahman, just as the space within a jug merges into absolute space when the walls of the jug are destroyed. Some few liberated souls have voluntarily returned to the world for a time to help others, but for the majority liberation means escape from the endless round of re-birth and suffering.

Even while he is alive the jivanmukta remains fully liberated. He can no longer see duality in the world; the problem that the world contains the mind and the mind contains the world, which we considered in Chapter IV, no longer exists for him. He sees all things in himself and himself in all things. This is not to say that liberation means the total liquidation or annihilation of the objective world: its disappearance is a purely metaphysical one in relation to the liberated person. The world still makes itself felt on him; but he always is aware of the complete identification of the world with himself. When a traveller learns that a lake seen in the desert is a mirage, it still looks like water to him, but his evaluation of the lake is changed.

As long as there is one unliberated jiva on earth, the world will continue to be, and Ishvara, out of the boundless compassion which is his nature, will continue to rule the world and exert himself to help that jiva to realise Brahman.

To many, the loss of the ego in Shankara's Absolute may seem terrifying, and while the Absolute is seen only through words this will always be so. It is quite true that the Absolute Brahman is qualityless, immutable, devoid of property or colour, as well as incomprehensible and indescribable, and that a metaphysical "search in

the dark for a black cat that isn't there" cannot give
support or consolation. At best the Absolue is a light
shining in a dark abyss, giving little illumination and no
warmth. But this is not the whole story. We have to
return to the point we have made many times in this
little study — that Shankara's philosophy is no mere intellectual exercise. It is a weakness of the empirical mind
that without training it cannot grasp Reality. It is no
mere form of words to say that our miseries and fears
arise out of falsely identifying ourselves with the phenomenal world. For Shankara, the great words sat, chit,
anandam — absolute existence, absolute consciousness
and absolute bliss — which are the qualities exhibited
by the qualityless Brahman in the phenomenal world, are
not philosophical abstractions, or even religious dogmas;
they are something to strive for, the objects of prayer and
meditation.

To the still unliberated soul, liberation may well seem
terrifying, for it is in the nature of a death. But it is
a blissful and conscious death. It is the death of the fear
of death, and the birth of the realisation that death is a
lie, that our true Self is immortal. Admittedly, we must
give up the ego in which our petty pleasures reside; but
with it we give up our miseries. In other contexts we
surrender our ego-hood without fear to obtain things we
know to be worth while — in deep sleep, in the enjoyment of great art, in play, in small acts of compassion,
in making love to one deeply loved, we are momentarily
without our ego, and who would argue that we were
poorer for its loss? As Blake says, "Every kindness to
another is a little death in the Divine Image". Love for
the body, for the family, for the nation, for humanity,
for all living beings, for the entire universe; in this
ascending order the individual soul manifests the supreme
Brahman as avidya is progressively removed.

Is it practical for a European to try to follow this
philosophy? There is little point in reading about it as
an intellectual exercise; it is a thing to be practised, a
way of life, a means for coming to terms with life and
our fellow creatures without selling our souls to any political or other creed. It is not inconsistent with our duties as

citizens; indeed, Shankara enjoins that we should discharge those duties as well and cheerfully as we can. But we should say fairly that it is a way for the self-reliant and for the seekers, and even for such people it is difficult to practise the philosophy in isolation. One should seek, best of all, a traditional teacher — there are now a number of them about the world over — or failing that, one should gather together with other like-minded persons, or at least seek devotion to God and to our fellowmen in the service of an institution. The way will in no case be easy; but the reward will be great—the achievement of our ultimate liberation and union with our Creator.

WHEN HE PRODUCED THIS COUPLET, DID THE POET BRAG—OR DID HE MAKE A POINT

Slokardhena pravakshyami yad uktham granthkotibhi!
Brahma sathyam jagan mithya jivo Brahmaiva naparah:

"I will explain in half a stanza the substance of a crore of texts!

Brahman is Real; Universe an illusion; Jiva and Brahman are not disparate."

NOTE ON THE LIFE OF SHANKARA

There is no "historical" biography of Shankara in existence, and such material as there is about him is a mixture of fact, tradition, legend and sheer fantasy which nobody can, or will ever be able to, sort out. Readers of this book may, however, find it interesting to have a summary of some of the material about Shankara's life and times which has come down to us — partly as legend and partly in written documents. These notes cannot be regarded as either biography or history, but neither are they pure fairy tales, and even the miraculous parts of them — and the fact that such miraculous stories exist at all — have a significant bearing on Shankara's place in Indian history. It is equally significant to the Western student of philosophy that there are no such apocryphal tales about Leibnitz or Hume.

The presence of mythical stories in his biography is not, of course, a reason for dismissing Shankara's philosophy as mere superstition — although prejudiced critics of Christianity have often applied this non-sequitur to the miracles recounted in the Gospels. The criterion of soundness of an argument is universal logic, and the criterion of validity of a religious or philosophical ideal is the equally universal standard of intuitive perception. Moreover, the most hardened materialist admits in practice — however strenuously he may deny it in theory — that one cannot extract the essence out of everything in life by logic alone. Plato did not scruple to invent myths for the exposition of ideas which he realised could not be got into the framework of the syllogism. The Indian mind, too, has a myth-making tendency which clothes the bare bones of history with the full flesh of their poetic significance; and in a certain sense it is true that history does not live until it has turned into mythology. In the following sketch no attempt has been made to "undo the webs of penelope"; facts and myths — some of them not at all edifying, it must be admitted — are set out in the inextricable tangle in which they have come down to us.

One of the early 'biographies' of Shankara, by Vidyaranya (or at least attributed to him) is fairly typical of ancient Indian biographies. It is not even certain that Vidyaranya wrote it; and it is below his other works in literary quality. It has always been the fashion in India to attribute the writing (or writing down) of works to **somebody,** and in many cases the attributions must be erroneous. Worse than that, Vidyaranya's biography (like others) is full of miracles and supernatural tales of its subject, who is portrayed as no less than an incarnation of the god Shankara (Shiva), after whom he was named. The amount of spurious matter is so great that if it were all removed there would be some doubt whether Shankara ever existed. The following account is, however, based on Vidyaranya's work, with modifications to accord with the stronger traditions.

No knotty problem defy scholarship as do dates in early Indian history. Shankara's date is no exception. One of his biographers, Anandagiri, holds that he was born at Chidambaram in 44 B.C. and died in 12 B.C., but he is alone in his view. Telang places him in the 6th. Century A.D., and Sir R. G. Bandarkar believes he was born in 680 A.D., while Professor Keith takes him forward to the early 9th. Century A.D. Venkiteswara, who thinks that within a span of thirty-two years Shankara could not have achieved as much as he is said to have done, would have him live ninety-two years, from 805 A.D. to 897 A.D. The most popularly held view is that he was born in 788 A.D. and died in 820 A.D. at the age of thirty-two. Max Muller, Macdonnel, Pathok, Deussen, Radhakrishnan and many other scholars are inclined to accept these dates.

Shankara was born in a village near Kaladi on the west coast of India. This village is situated on the banks of the Churni, up the Alwaye River, and is six miles from Alwaye, now a station on the Cochin-Shoranur railway line. During Shankara's life-time, Kaladi belonged to Cochin.

Shankara was a member of the Nambudiri or Malabar class of Vedic Brahmins, an exclusive sect, and his father and mother were Shivaguru and Aryamba. They remained childless for long and, it is said, invoked at last the help of their family deity, Shiva. One night, Shiva appeared to Aryamba in a dream and asked whether she would prefer a long-lived dunderhead or a short-lived genius for a son. In her wisdom, Aryamba chose the genius. Anandagiri says that at that time Shiva himself, at the instance of the heavenly powers, was eager to be born on earth for the resuscitation of the decaying Vedic culture; and, after blessing Aryamba, himself entered her womb to be born as Shankara.

Shankara's father died when he was but seven, by which time he had already sarted learning the alphabets. The "investiture of the sacred thread" had consequent to the bereavement, to be postponed and was later conducted by his mother. We are told that within a year the boy, showing amazing talent and precocity, had mastered the Vedas and returned to his mother from the teacher's home. Already a number of parents with eligible daughters had started soliciting Aryamba for her son, but she was reminded — so it is said — by the sage Agasthya that Shankara was to die young, being the wise but short-lived child that she had chosen from Shiva.

Shankara was already developing a keen desire to take to the life of asceticism. This appears to have been a sad blow to Aryamba, widowed as she was, and she bewailed the prospect that there would be none now to perform her funeral rites. Shankara promised her that, although it was contrary to the conventional rules of the ascetic order, he would perform her obsequies and care for her soul.

There is a legend that Shankara employed a ruse to obtain her consent. Aryamba and Shankara had gone to bathe in the river, which was in flood, and Shankara, plunging into the water, suddenly cried out, "A crocodile has got me, Mother! I am going! But at this moment of death, let my soul be saved — let me die an ascetic

— I shall then be at peace!" Whether he was literally
attacked by a crocodile, or whether the crocodile was
merely a symbol for the worldly life — which in the
Indian classics is often likened to a river infested with
crocodiles — is hard to say. However it was, his mother
gave her consent, albeit reluctantly, and having secured
her permission to go in for the most extreme form of
the ascetic's life, Shankara found himself freed from the
clutches of the crocodile, which vanished as mysteriously
as it had appeared.

Shankara now left home in search of a teacher who
would formally initiate him into the holy order of Sannyasa. India was then, as ever, rich in seats of learning
presided over by austere scholars, and to one of these,
on the banks of the Narmada, Shankara was led. The
teacher here was a great ascetic named Govinda, whom
Shankara came to revere immensely, and to whom he
pays homage in nearly all his works, as also to his teacher's teacher, Gaudapada. Tradition has it that the
temple at Badari was subsequently built in commemora-
tion of Shankara's initiation here.

After his course of instruction, Shankara was advised
to become a peripatetic teacher of religion, and he set
off for Benares, which was a great centre of learning and
abounded in philosophers and dialectitians. In spite of
his youth, the new arrival was soon outstanding, so acute
was his intellect, so complete his mastery of the Vedas
and other scriptural texts, and the various systems of
philosophy. He attracted many pupils, the most not-
able of whom was a novice who later came to be known
as Padmapada. This name was given to him, we are
told, because of the following incident. Once when Shankara and his pupil found themselves on opposite banks
of the River Ganges in flood, Shankara beckoned to his
pupil to come to him, and he, with complete faith, step-
ped onto the water and walked over the river as if on
dry land. And it is said that at every step he took a
padma (lotus) blossomed to support his pada (foot).

Shankara then spent some years at Benares and
Badari, devoting his time mainly to the writing of the
various commentaries for which he is famous, and, in

consultation with men of repute there, perfecting them
One tradition has it that his first work was his well-known
commentary on the Brahma Sutras in his twelfth
year, and that this was followed by his commentaries on the ten leading Upanishads. Another and
more popular view is that he began his writing in
Benares with a commentary on the thousand names of
Vishnu, known as the Vishnusahasranama, and that the
commentaries on the Upanishads, the Bhagavad Gita and
the Brahma Sutras came later. Modern scholars, however, are inclined on internal evidence of style to doubt
Shankara's authorship of the Vishnusahasranama.

Tradition, by way of a legend, again has hinted at certain differences that exist between the fundamental teachings of the Brahma Sutras themselves and the doctrine
Shankara developed through his commentary on the
Sutras. The legend is that Vyasa, the reputed author of
the Brahma Sutras, assumed the guise of an old man,
called on Shankara, and entered into a disputation with
him which lasted several days and threatened to last for
ever. Padmapada thereupon begged that the incarnations
of Shiva (obvious reference to Shankara) and Vishnu
(reference to Vyasa) should end the controversy. One may
gather from this story the fact that the Brahma Sutras
had been traditionally interpreted in other than the ab-
solutist method adopted by Shankara, and that Shankara
had to meet in argument a champion of his other interpretation who was his equal in dialectics as well as in
the mastery of the Sutras. The story ends with an ad-
mission from the distinguished Vyasa that, although he
and Shankara differed in their interpretation, Shankara's
was finer and more profound.

Now, although Shankara himself had had a sound spiritual education under a traditional teacher, the period
in which he was born was one of intellectual chaos and
spiritual degeneration. Religions based on mere rituals,
formulae and sacrifices flourished, and the followers of
Buddha himself had reduced their philosophy to that
empty nothingness still often unjustly attributed to the
genuine doctrine of that great teacher. Monasteries had
become breeding-places of quack philosophers and

pseudo-mystics, engaged in senseless polemics with vedic ritualists and other schools of philosophy. Young aspirants to priesthood were ill-taught and lost in an ocean of book-learning. Logic and logomachy were the sole aim.

All this Shankara condemned and worked to reform. Listening one day to the irritating sound of a religious student at Benares learning a text of Sanskrit grammar by rote, Shankara — so tradition has it — broke out extempore into a song of twelve verses with the refrain, "Worship Govinda, the Preserver, you fool! When you are face to face with death at the appointed time, grammatical formulae cannot save you!"

Besides attacking the false methods of education and philosophy, Shankara turned his attention to the many and varying sects then in existence, which, while differing widely in many respects, agreed in one — that of indulgence in ceremonies of an abominable nature. So effective were Shankara's attacks that he practically wiped them out; although, uncompromising champion of the philosophy of non-dualism as he was, he was not a persecuting officer of a church militant. He realised that his doctrines were bound to remain caviare to the general. He was tolerant and alive to the frailties of human nature, and because he was aware that the ordinary mind could not attain to the heights of his philosophy, he adopted methods which, though tantamount to a compromise with lesser faiths, were calculated to lead the people at a lower stage of spiritual knowledge step by step from the "lower" to the "higher" knowledge. It is a tribute to this broad outlook and tolerance that he is known also as "the founder of six faiths". The bulk of the people then worshipped one or other of the following five deities: the Sun, Ambika (or Shakti), Vishnu, Ganapathy and Shiva. Shankara persuaded the people to worship all five deities as an aid to their spiritual growth, and so laid the foundations of unity among the sects — the important thing being not so much the outward observance as the effect of worship on the devotee's progress towards his real spiritual goal. He moreover wrote a poem of five stanzas proclaiming that "the man of non-dual realisation, be he a brahmin or a chandala (swee-per) is my teacher".

But to return to Shankara's life. He now left Benares on a country-wide tour, accompanied by several pupils and much paraphernalia. This bears testimony to his fame and popularity, which is said to have brought him the patronage of several royal personages and chiefs, and in the end his travels earned him the title of "the best of peripatetic teachers". His first stop was at Allahabad and while resting here, he heard that the famous cham-pion of the Purva Mimamsa school and an inveterate enemy of Buddhism, Kumarila Bhatta, was proposing to burn himself.

Bhatta was an Assamese Brahmin who had been edu-cated under a Buddhist teacher. As a Brahmin, his faith in the revealed truth and supreme authority of the Vedas was too deep-rooted to allow of any other philosophy alien or hostile to the Vedas to claim absolute allegiance. He could not even bear any criticism of the Vedas from his teacher. His fellow-students, noticing the change that had come over him, concluded him to be a heretic and made several attempts on his life. His miraculous esca-pes from death won him the patronage of King Sudhan-van until then a follower of Buddhism, and together they started a nation-wide campaign against the Buddhists. Large conversions from Buddhism to Vedism resulted, and Bhatta gained a wide following in the country. Two things seem, however, to have haunted him, driving him finally to chasten himself by burning. These were the destruction of his teacher "in the flame of persecution which he himself kindled", and "the practical denial of God in his endeavour to prove the absolute revelational character of the Vedas and the sole efficacy of the Vedic rites to save men".

Hearing of Bhatta's intended self-immolation, Shan-kara rushed to him but arrived to find Bhatta already in flames. Shankara asked for the pleasure of a debate with him, but since Bhatta was half-burnt and no longer able to express himself freely, he merely gave Shankara the name of his brother-in-law and pupil, Mandana Misra, who lived at Mahishamati.

There are difficulties in accepting this alleged encounter of Shankara with Kumarila Bhatta, for we have independent evidence for the belief that the latter lived in the second half of the .7th. century A.D. It is, however, certain that he did meet and defeat in argument Mandana Misra. This Mandana Misra was probably not the same person as the brother-in-law and disciple of Bhatta, though belonging to the same doctrinal school.

Shankara set off now to meet Mandana, who at that time was chief pundit (chief minister) at the Court at Mahishamati, leading a life of prodigal luxury. The story goes that Shankara, finding the door bolted, entered the house mysteriously, to find a crowd of men and women servants and rows of parrots all repeating their master's dogmatic formula. Mandana himself was engaged in a consecration ceremony, and, seeing a man enter who belonged to the ascetic order which he despised, he burst into a violent temper. A facetious conversation ensued, until the Brahmins who were present intervened and stopped it.

There followed a full-fledged disputation at which Bharati, the learned wife of Mandana, was asked to umpire. (Bharati is said to be an incarnation of Saraswati, the goddess of learning, who had taken human form to atone for the sin of laughing at sage Durvasa over an omission he made while reciting the Vedas in the Court of Brahma, her husband). Learned scholar as she was reputed to be, she did not remain during the whole of the debate, but is said to have thrown a garland over the shoulders of each contestant, declaring that he whose garland first showed sings of fading should own defeat and accept the other's creed. The disputation lasted seventeen days, and, at last, Kandana's garland began to fade. He kept his word and agreed to accept the red robes of the ascetic order and follow Shankara. Bharati, now that her husband was to all purposes dead to her, was preparing to leave the house, when Shankara asked her if she, too, would debate with him (although according to another version it was Bharati who insisted on this — arguing that he had only defeated one half of Mandana; Shankara is reported to have objected that he could not discourse with women, but Bharati could cite scriptural sanctions against him, so that he was forced to agree to the debate). Thus it was that a second disputation began, lasting another seventeen days. Finding Shankara unbeatable, Bharati, perhaps in despair, challenged him on a discussion of the Kama Shastra, or science of eroticism. Obviously, Shankara, the ascetic, could not meet her on this ground, but, refusing to own defeat, begged for a postponement of one month in which to prepare himself for the argument. This was granted and Shankara departed.

Setting off on this journey with his disciples, Shankara met a funeral procession in which the body of King Amaru was being carried for cremation. Shankara promptly used his magical powers, and, after instructing his pupils to keep watch over his body lying in a hollow tree, he separated his soul from the body and entered that of the king. There followed a general rejoicing at what was thought to be the king's resurrection, no one suspecting the transformation.

The luxurious life and the blandishments of the queens, as well as his onerous duties of state, made Shankara forget his promise of return within a month. Moreover, his genius in the management of affairs was arousing doubts among the ministers as to his identity. Yogic powers were suspected, and it was decided to search the neighbourhood for the body of any yogi who might have played the trick of entering the king's body. Shankara's body was soon discovered in the hollow tree, and preparations were made to burn it surreptitiously. Meanwhile, Shankara's failure to return at the appointed time had aroused fears in the minds of the pupils who had custody of his body, and they had set out in search of his soul. Hearing the news of King Amaru's resurrection, they had gone to his Court to investigate, and there had succeeded in reviving Shankara's memory by singing to him some of his favourite songs. Shankara's soul immediately left the king's body and hurried back to find his own, only to discover that the court messengers had already set it on fire. He nevertheless entered the body, and sang the praises of Vishnu, invoking his powers to produce rain and put out the fire. The rain came, and Shankara's body was saved for his further use.

During his life at the Court, Shankara is said to have written a work on erotics, recording his experiences with the queens. This work still exists, but scholars repudiate that it could have been written by the author of the commentaries. (But John Donne's sermons were written by the author of "On his Mistris Going to Bed".)

Shankara now returned to Bharati, and, having satisfied her that he was master even of the art of love, established his omniscience. Some say that Bharati then left for her heavenly abode, but others that she too followed Shankara and eventually spent the rest of her life at Sringeri, where Shankara established a college, at the head of which he placed the defeated Mandana. This conversion of Bharati and her decision to serve her husband, not as husband now but as a spiritual teacher, is understandable if we remember that at this period women were not yet driven into the seclusion of purdah but still enjoyed intellectual freedom and a considerable choice of action. Certain it is that Shankara greatly esteemed a lady named Bharati, as the temple erected to her memory at Sringeri bears witness.

From Mahishamati, Shankara went south. While passing through Maharashtra he nearly fell a victim to a fanatic of the notorious Kapalika sect, who worshipped Bhairava, the Destroyer, who demanded human sacrifices and was alleged to have a partiality for the heads of learned Brahmins. While Shankara was absorbed in deep contemplation in a lonely spot, this Kapalika found him and was about to kill him with an axe, when Padmapada fortunately arrived and killed the fanatic before his axe could fall on Shankara.

Shankara's next stop was at the place now known as Sringeri, on the banks of the Tungabhadra, where he built the temple dedicated to the goddess of learning and also set up a college. To this day, this college has remained one of the most honoured religious institutions in India. Although travel to Sringeri is still a tedious process, it does attract a multitude of devotees from among Hindus and Muslims. Even the militant Tippu Sultan was a devoted votary of the temple at Sringeri, and presented costly ornaments, including a large, green emerald of inestimable value to adorn the idol.

At Sringeri, Shankara is said to have expressed the desire that a gloss should be added to his commentary on the Brahma Sutras and suggested that Mandana, because of his scholarship and intimate knowledge of the Karma Kanda philosophy, should undertake it. His pupils, jealous of the new convert and his intimacy with the master, put forward Padmapada, on the grounds that there was no real evidence of a change of heart in Mandana, whose adherence to the new philosophy could be ascribed merely to his defeat in the controversy. They hinted that Mandana might, by introducing subversive material into the gloss, sabotage the doctrine of non-dualism. Padmapada, on the other hand, was completely trustworthy. Shankara yielded and gave the work to Padmapada, allotting to Mandana as consolation the annotation of his commentaries on the Upanishads.

After completing his gloss on the Brahma Sutras commentary, Padmapada asked for permission to go to Rameswaram on a short visit, and this was granted. He set off, taking with him the manuscript on which he had been working. His first call was on his uncle, who was a follower of the Karma Kanda school, at Chidambaram, leaving there the manuscript for safe custody, and then proceeding to Rameswaram. During his newphew's absence, the uncle learning of the contents of the manuscript and realising that they were hostile to his own school of thought, staged a fire in which the book was destroyed. Padmapada, on his return, was horrified at the loss, which he thought he could never repair; for his uncle not content with destroying the manuscript, even gave his nephew a drug to injure his mind. Padmapada returned to Shankara and confessed the loss, but his master at once consoled him and dictated the contents of the burned record from memory. Neither the original nor the reproduced version of this glossary has come down to us.

It was during Padmapada's absence on leave that Shankara received news of his mother's illness and went to see her. On meeting her, we are told, he touched her feet in reverence — his first overt act of defiance to the ascetic rules. His mother, realising that she was about to die, begged her son to talk to her of divine grace, so that she might obtain salvation. Shankara, forgetting that she was simple and uneducated, discoursed to her pedantically on the doctrine of non-dualism; she told him to spare her his learnedness and talk only of that which she could comprehend. Shankara then sang her an impromptu hymn to Shiva; Shiva's messengers appeared, to collect her soul, but they frightened her, and when she appealed to her son, he sang again, this time in praise of Vishnu, whose messengers, less fearful, came to replace the messengers of Shiva. Finally, Aryamba blessed her son and left the world.

In accordance with his promise given to her long ago, Shankara proceeded to carry out the funeral rites, although this was prohibited to an ascetic by the rules of his order. Thus for the second time Shankara defied convention, bringing down on himself the wrath of a jealous community. They refused him any help, even withholding firewood for the funeral pyre. Some have criticised Shankara for infringing so blatantly the rules of his order, but it would surely seem that such an action as his is to be admired. An ascetic renounces desires and passions, but he does not renounce nobility and decency. Shankara put filial affection above dogma, and who can deny that it adds to his stature?

The hostility of the community did not deter Shankara from his course of duty. Unable to carry his mother's corpse alone, he cut it into pieces and carried them to the back-yard of the house, where, using yogic powers, he managed to built a pyre from the only material available — the green stems of plantain trees.

After the funeral and the attendant obsequies, Shankara decided to teach the community who had acted so petulantly a lesson that succeeding generations would not forget. He therefore induced the local chief to forbid them, by an edict, to chant the Vedas. They were also compelled to cremate their dead within the compounds of their houses — illams, as they are called — a further stipulation being that the bodies should be mutilated before being cremated.

Parenthetically, it might here be added that the Malabar Brahmins have continued to our day the practice not only of cremating their dead within their own compounds but also of symbolically mangling the corpses before burning by touching the joints of the body with a knife made for the purpose. Moreover, they explain their practices by quoting scriptures which refer to the curse that Shankara pronounced following the death and cremation of his mother. Pazurpanai Illam, a house in a suburb of Trichur in Kerala, is popularly held to have been the house to which Shankara's mother belonged, and a place within its compound is pointed out as the spot where she was cremated.

Shankara now returned to Sringeri, collected his pupils, and left on his all-India tour. In the course of a stay at Puri, he set up an institution there known as Govardhan College, which has flourished to this day. We are told also that, during this period of tour in the south, the kings of Chola and Pandya were converted to Shankara's philosophy and that they took him under their royal patronage.

At Ujjain, which appears to have been Shankara's next halt, he came to grips with the Saiva sect, known as Bhairavas, who indulged in human sacrifices. Having won over the local chieftains, partly by argument and, when that failed, by force, he succeeded in suppressing this sect, which was headed by a cruel tyrant called Krakaea — literally, a saw — thus putting a stop to their atrocities.

Shankara then toured Gurjaradesa, establishing another college at Dwaraka. After this, following the course of the Ganges, he travelled east. During this part of his journey, he won many victories over his critics and over followers of rival schools. In Kashmir, which seethed with Buddhist dialecticians, he crushed in argument all who ventured to face him and ascended the famous Seat of Learning.

We now come to practically the last days of Shankara. Here we get a vague glimpse of his tour of Bengal and Assam. It was at Gauhati, in Assam, that he is said to have met the formidable champion of the Sakta cult, Abhinava Gupta, and defeated him in a controversy. Gupta, unable to accept defeat gracefully, is accused of having cast an evil spell on his rival, causing him to fall ill with haemorrhoids. All the doctors who were called in failed to cure him. Then Padmapada, to whom a messenger from Shiva is said to have revealed the cause of the disease, invoked his own knowledge of black magic, and, by neutralising Gupta's spells, cured Shankara.

But Shankara did not live long thereafter. He went on to Badri and there established a college, also building a temple to Narayana. Then he retired to Kedarnath, where, at the age of thirty-two, he entered a cave to achieve the fourth state of consciousness, samadhi, and did not return.

The picture of Shankara's life which we see, thus mistily, through the words of "biographers" and the living tradition of India may bear more resemblance to the truth — notwithstanding the grotesque trappings — than one is inclined at first sight to think possible. But it is no great matter who he was as an earthly individual. The important thing is that his works should ever have been written, and it is a sufficient enough miracle that simple people should have thought it worth while weaving any myths at all around their author. It is as though Englishmen were to have a strong living tradition of the life of the unknown author of the "Cloud of Unknowing" and to be still learning in colleges which he founded.

Moreover, whatever may or may not be deduced from them about his life, the literary quality of his work speaks for itself. It is impossible for all but a few to become Sanskrit scholars, and any translation of Shankara's work is therefore bound to sacrifice the poetic quality of the original, but those who can read Sanskrit are unanimous that his diction has a simplicity and directness, a literary freshness; and that his writings are matchless for "compass and power and charm". They are informed by a wisdom which "reacheth from end to end, sweetly and strongly ordering all things". At once serene and humorous, they appeal to the head as well as to the heart. By using those metaphors from simple everyday peasant life which adorn the style of much Indian philosophy, Shankara turns the abstruse into the simple and brings the recondite within the range of the student who has no exceptional powers.

As seen through his works, the Acharya — the "Master" — shines in the Indian philosophical sky as a luminary of the first magnitude. Whoever he was, and whenever he lived, he was something more than a clever intellectual. It is hard to believe that in his day he was anything less than the most inspiring teacher and preacher who had appeared since the time of Buddha, and we can see him as a personality at once profound and simple, learned but human, belonging to this world but also to that greater world which the Indian philosophers have always recognized as a single unity with the deity in the innermost heart of man.

THE MIND OF SWAMI VIVEKANANDA
by Gautam Sen

Swami Vivekananda was one of the great religious minds of the 19th century. His appearance before the Congress of World Religions in America was a momentous event in the history of religion. Here, he forever changed the Western view of Vedanta and Hindu philosophy. What was hitherto considered an assortment of superstitions was revealed by Vivekananda's eloquence to be a sophisticated religious and metaphysical system which won the respect of Western thinkers.

What is the substance of Vivekananda's interpretation of Vedanta? And how relevant is it to 20th Century man? In this volume Gautam Sen pieces together the representative portions of the Swami's philosophy and ties them up with a running commentary of his own.

THE MIND OF J. KRISHNAMURTI
Edited by Luis S R. Vas

The world is in a state of perpetual flux. Nothing is permanent any longer, change is everywhere. Its effects have been devastating on the fabric of human life and society. How does one come to grips with the situation?

J. Krishnamurti has the answer: self-knowledge—a process as deceptively simple and wonderful as opening one's eyes to the full beauty of life. But most of us have forgotten the use of eye-lids and are blind by choice.

Krishnamurti's influence on Aldous Huxley and Alan Watts has been deep. Yet he addresses himself chiefly to the common man, not to the professional philosopher.

In this volume over fifty articles, conversations and aphorisms have been collected. They represent the most comprehensive study available of the renowned non-Guru.

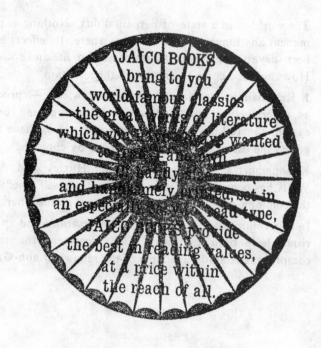

COMPLETE
JAICO CATALOGUE

ORIENTAL CLASSICS

J-1   THE RUBAIYAT   Rs. 25
       OF OMAR KHAYYAM

J-3   PANCHATANTRA   Rs. 55

J-72   JATAKA TALES   Rs. 50

J-242   THE RAMAYANA   Rs. 12

J-243   THE MAHABHARATA   Rs. 13

-477   THE PROPHET   Rs.25/-

J-519   KING VIKRAM & THE   Rs. 36
        GHOST

J-532   TALES FROM 1001   Rs. 150
        ARABIAN NIGHTS

J-545 IMMORTAL TALES FROM KALIDASA — Rs. 32

J-547 THE GREAT THRONE OF KING VIKRAMADITYA — Rs. 15

J-611 MAHABHARATA (II PARTS) — Rs. 25 Per Set

J-611 MAHABHARATA (II PARTS) — Rs. 25 Per Set

J-666 RAMAYANA OF GOSWAMI TULSIDAS — Rs. 85

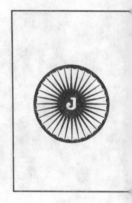

INDIAN LITERATURE

J-26 THE GOLDEN BOAT — Rs. 25

J-27 NECTAR IN A SIEVE — Rs. 26

J-42 FAREWELL MY   Rs. 30
       FRIEND & THE GARDEN

J-52 GODAN   Rs. 45

J-207 CHEMMEEN   Rs. 25

J-264 POSSESSION   Rs. 15

J-317 OUR UNIVERSE   Rs. 25

J-318 LIPIKA   Rs. 25

J-339 SRIKANTA.   Rs. 20

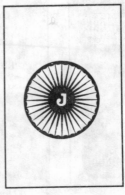

WESTERN
LITERATURE

khalil gibran
reader

SPIRITS REBELLIOUS

SECRETS OF THE HEART

TEARS AND LAUGHTER

J-439   THE KHALIL GIBRAN   Rs. 55
        READER

P.G. WODEHOUSE

The Head of Kay's

J-490   THE HEAD OF KAY'S   Rs. 25

P.G. WODEHOUSE

The Pothunters

J-491   THE POTHUNTERS   Rs. 24

P.G. WODEHOUSE

A Prefect's Uncle

J-492   A PREFECT'S UNCLE   Rs. 24

P.G. WODEHOUSE

The White Feather

J-493   THE WHITE FEATHER   Rs. 25

P.G. WODEHOUSE

The Gold Bat

J-494   THE GOLD BAT   Rs. 25

Robert Louis Stevenson
JAICO CLASSICS SERIES

Kidnapped

J-511   KIDNAPPED   Rs. 15

Daniel Defoe
JAICO CLASSICS SERIES

The Life and Adventures of
Robinson Crusoe

J-512   THE ADVENTURES   Rs. 15
        OF ROBINSON CRUSOE

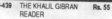

J-513 20,000 LEAGUES   Rs. 15
UNDER THE SEA

J-514 AROUND THE WORLD   Rs. 15
IN EIGHTY DAYS

J-520 THE COMPLETE LONG   Rs. 65
STORIES OF SHERLOCK
HOLMES

J-522 THE COUNT OF   Rs. 15
MONTE CRISTO

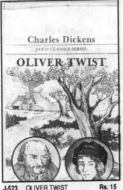

J-523 OLIVER TWIST   Rs. 15

J-524 THE ADVENTURES   Rs. 15
OF SHERLOCK HOLMES

J-525 THE STRANGE CASE   Rs. 15
OF DR. JEKYLL &
MR. HYDE

J-526 DAVID COPPERFIELD   Rs. 15

J-527 TREASURE ISLAND   Rs. 15

J-528   THE ADVENTURES OF   **Rs. 15**
TOM SAWYER

J-529   THE MAN IN THE IRON   **Rs. 15**
MASK

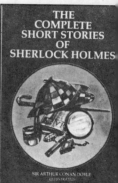

J-530   THE COMPLETE   **Rs. 135**
SHORT STORIES OF
SHERLOCK HOLMES

J-544   LADY CHATTERLEY'S   **Rs. 40**
LOVER

J-548   A TALE OF TWO CITIES   **Rs. 15**

J-551   THE HOUND OF   **Rs. 15**
BASKERVILLES

J-568   THE HUNCHBACK OF   **Rs. 15**
NOTRE-DAME

J-572   THE PRISONER OF   **Rs. 15**
ZENDA

J-573   ADVENTURES OF   **Rs. 15**
ROBIN HOOD

J-586 THE GREATEST Rs. 180
WORKS OF KAHLIL GIBRAN

J-595 IVANHOE Rs. 15

J-598 THE WORLD'S Rs. 130
GREATEST SHORT STORIES

J-602 HIS LAST BOW Rs. 35

J-603 THE CASE-BOOK OF Rs. 35
SHERLOCK HOLMES

J-604 THE MEMOIRS OF Rs. 35
SHERLOCK HOLMES

J-605 THE ADVENTURES OF Rs. 35
SHERLOCK HOLMES

J-606 THE RETURN OF Rs. 35
SHERLOCK HOLMES

J-616 ADVENTURES OF DON Rs. 15
QUIXOTE

J-639 THE INVISIBLE MAN — Rs. 15

J-644 THE BOOK OF GREAT Rs. 150
MYSTERIES

J-694 THE WORLD'S Rs. 175
GREATEST LOVE STORIES

JB-522 THE COUNT OF Rs. 15
MONTE CRISTO (BENGALI)

JB-525 THE STRANGE CASE Rs. 15
OF DR. JEKYLL &
MR. HYDE (BENGALI)

JB-548 A TALE OF TWO CITIES Rs. 15
(BENGALI)

JB-573 ADVENTURES OF Rs. 15
ROBINHOOD (BENGALI)

JB-616 ADVENTURES OF DON Rs. 15
QUIXOTE (BENGALI)

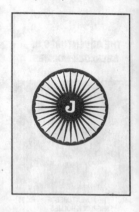

AUTOBIOGRAPHIES AND BIOGRAPHIES

J-41 MAHATMA GANDHI **Rs. 75**
(ESSAYS & REFLECTIONS)

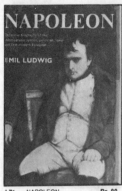

J-71 NAPOLEON **Rs. 80**

J-142 JAWAHARLAL NEHRU **TOP**

J-175 SUBHASH CHANDRA **Rs. 45**
BOSE

J-196 AUTOBIOGRAPHY **Rs. 46**
OF A YOGI (ENGLISH)

J-196 YOGI KATHAMRIT **Rs. 50**
(HINDI)

JT-196 YOGI ATMAKATHA **Rs. 65**
(TELGU)

J-208 AUTOBIOGRAPHY OF **Rs. 75**
AN UNKNOWN INDIAN

J-316   A TAGORE   **Rs. 30**
TESTAMENT

J-412   ADOLF HITLER   **Rs. 35**

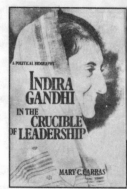

J-475   INDIRA GANDHI IN   **Rs. 175 (HB)**
THE CRUCIBLE OF   **Rs. 15 (HB)**
LEADERSHIP

J-510   MEJDA: SRI PARAMA-   **Rs. 40**
HANSA YOGANANDA -
HIS FAMILY & EARLY LIFE

J-541   MEIN KAMPF   **Rs. 125**

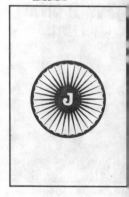

HISTORY, POLITICS
AND
SOCIOLOGY

J-247   THE CONTINENT OF   **Rs. 60**
CIRCE

J-464   WAR OF THE   **Rs. 20**
SPRINGING TIGERS

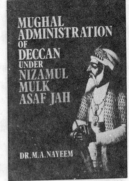

JH-38	HOW MOSCOW	Rs. 40(PB)
JH-53	SEES KASHMIR	Rs. 125(HB)

JH-58 PRINCELY INDIA & Rs. 220
LAPSE OF BRITISH
PARAMOUNTCY

JH-59 MUGHAL ADMINIS- Rs. 300
TRATION OF DECCAN UNDER
NIZAMUL MULK ASAF JAH

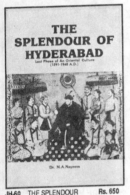

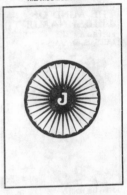

JH-60 THE SPLENDOUR Rs. 650
OF HYDERABAD

JH-67 THE RANI OF JHANSI Rs. 200

J-33 THE WISDOM OF INDIA Rs. 75

J-64 THE SONG CELESTIAL Rs. 35
BHAGAVAD GITA

J-124   GLIMPSES OF WORLD   Rs. 55
         RELIGIONS

J-126   RAMANA MAHARSHI   Rs. 45
         THE PATH OF SELF-
         KNOWLEDGE

J-176   THE IMPORTANCE OF   TOP
         LIVING

J-363   THE MIND OF   Rs. 55
         J. KRISHNAMURTI

J-384   THE BASIC WRITINGS   Rs. 40
         OF S. RADHAKRISHNAN

J-411   THE MIND OF   Rs. 35
         SWAMI VIVEKANANDA

J-429   BEGONE GODMEN   Rs. 35

J-430   THE MIND OF   Rs. 30
         ADI SHAKARACHARYA

J-452   GODS, DEMONS &   Rs. 40
         SPIRITS

J-482 KRISHNA: MYTH OR REALITY — Rs. 12

J-506 THE BHAGAVATAM — TOP

J-574 KRISHNA : THE MAN & HIS PHILOSOPHY — Rs. 140

J-488 SAGES & SAINTS OF INDIA — TOP

J-509 TREASURY OF SPIRITUAL TRUTHS — Rs. 20

J-600 HINDU PHILOSOPHY — Rs. 45

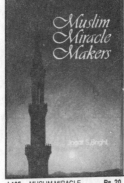

J-495 MUSLIM MIRACLE MAKERS — Rs. 20

J-557 UNDERSTANDING PHILOSOPHY — Rs. 45

J-661 SAI BABA OF SHIRDI — Rs.110

LAW & CRIME

J-561 FUTURE CRIME   Rs. 35

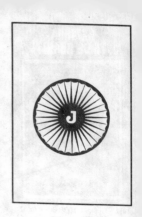

BUSINESS, MANAGEMENT & ECONOMICS

J-460 HOW TO FIGHT DIRTY   Rs.40
AGAINST MANAGEMENT

J-462 HOW TO CUT   Rs. 40
OFFICE COSTS

J-515 THE MAGIC OF RATIOS   Rs. 35

J-531 BACK TO BASICS: Rs. 35
PLANNING

J-533 YOU CAN NEGOTIATE   Rs. 60
ANYTHING

CORPORATE COMBAT
The Application of Military Strategy and Tactics to Business Competition

William Peacock

J-534   CORPORATE COMBAT   Rs. 40

Industrial **Purchasing** And **Materials Management**

H.L. Chadha

J-538   INDUSTRIAL PURC-   Rs. 75
HASE ING& MATERIALS
MANAGEMENT

Accounting And Finance For Managers

B.K. Chatterjee

J-539   ACCOUNTING &   Rs.140
FINANCE FOR MANAGERS

THE CREDIT REPORT

RAGHU R. PALAT

J-543   THE CREDIT REPORT   Rs. 35

MATERIALS MANAGEMENT AND INVENTORY CONTROL

J-546   MATERIALS MANA-   Rs.75(PB)
JH-69   GEMENT & INVEN-   Rs.195 (HB)
TORY CONTROL

Tax Planning For The Salaried Employee

Raghu R. Palat

J-720   TAX PLANNING FOR   Rs. 40
THE SALARIED EMPLOYEE
(Revised Edition 1993/94)

THE GREATEST MANAGEMENT PRINCIPLE IN THE WORLD

GMP

MICHAEL Le BOEUF
Ph. D.

J-550   THE GREATEST   Rs.35
MANAGEMENT PRINCIPLE

MANAGEMENT BY COMMONSENSE

T. GOKULAN

J-559   MANAGEMENT BY   Rs. 55
COMMON SENSE

PROMOTING SALES

J-567   PROMOTING SALES   Rs. 40

THE LAST WORD ON MANAGEMENT

A COLLECTION OF QUOTATIONS THAT OFFER THE ULTIMATE WISDOM

ROLF B. WHITE

J-570 THE LAST WORD ON MANAGEMENT   **Rs. 55**

FINANCE FOR NON-FINANCE MANAGERS
B.K. CHATTERJEE

J-587 FINANCE FOR NON-FINANCE MANAGERS   **Rs. 75**

COSTING AND MANAGERIAL ACCOUNTING FOR MANAGERS

J-588 COSTING & MANAGERIAL ACCOUNTING   **Rs. 80**

HOW TO READ ANNUAL REPORTS AND BALANCE SHEETS

RAGHU R. PALAT

J-617 HOW TO READ ANNUAL REPORTS   **Rs. 65**

TELEMARKETING THAT WORKS

How To Create A Winning Program For Your Company

J-634 TELEMARKETING THAT WORKS   **Rs. 90**

UNLOCKING CREATIVITY IN THE WORKPLACE

Grossman, Rodgers & Moore

J-656 UNLOCKING CREATIVITY   **Rs. 60**

STEPS TO STRATEGIC MANAGEMENT
A Guide for Entrepreneurs

J-657 STEPS TO STRATEGIC MANAGEMENT   **Rs. 55**

THE ACTION-CENTRED LEADER

J-662 THE ACTION CENTRED LEADER   **Rs. 50**

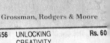

The Effective Supervisor

John Adair

J-664 THE EFFECTIVE SUPERVISOR   **Rs. 50**

J-78 TECHNIQUES OF FINANCIAL ANALYSIS Rs. 120

J-695 OTC EXCHANGE OF INDIA Rs. 50

J-734 JAICO'S WONDER WORLD OF INVESTMENTS (Revised Edition 1993/94)

J-735 A COMPLETE GUIDE FOR NON-RESIDENT INDIANS (1993/94) Rs. 80

J-696 COMPENSATING YOUR SALES FORCE Rs. 90

JH-7 HANDBOOK OF SERVICE CONDITIONS FOR WORKMEN IN BANKS Rs. 60

JH-24 PERSONNEL MANAGEMENT Rs. 55

JH-43 PERSONNEL MANAGEMENT-AN OVERVIEW Rs. 30

JH-45 MARKETING MANAGEMENT : A FINANCE EMPHASIS Rs. 75

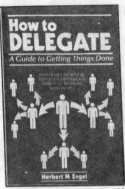

JH-55 HOW TO DELEGATE- Rs. 160 (HB)
A GUIDE TO GETTING (Rs. 65 (PB)
THINGS DONE

JH-56 NON-RESIDENTS : TAX- Rs. 350
ATION & INVESTMENT
IN INDIA

JH-57 THE NEW MANAGE- Rs. 200 (HB)
RIAL GRID Rs. 75 (PB)

JH-63 GEMS OF Rs. 200 (HB)
MANAGEMENT Rs. 55 (PB)

JH-65 AN EXECUTIVE'S Rs. 225
COACHING HAND BOOK

JH-66 SOCIAL VIEW OF Rs. 17_
INDUSTRIAL RELATIONS

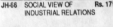

JH-68 PROUT & ECONOMIC Rs. 150
REFORM IN INDIA &
THE THIRD WORLD

JH-74 THE MAKINGS OF A Rs. 200
MILLIONAIRE

JH-75 ZERO BASE PRICING Rs. 41_

JH-79 IMPROVING ORGANISATIONAL EFFECTIVENESS — Rs. 250

JH-80 THE ART & SCIENCE OF BUSINESS MANAGEMENT (in 7 Vols.) — Rs. 3500 (Per Set)

JH-86 THE STRUGGLE TO SURVIVE IN THE THIRD WORLD — Rs. 225

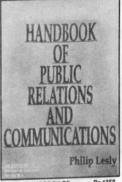

JH-87 PROJECT COST CONTROL FOR MANAGERS — Rs. 300

JH-88A COST REDUCTION HANDBOOK — Rs. 650

JH-90 HANDBOOK OF PUBLIC RELATIONS & COMMUNICATIONS — Rs.1350

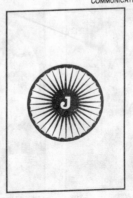

JH-91 SAFETY MANAGEMENT IN INDUSTRY — Rs. 975

BOOKS FOR EVERYDAY USE

J-372 WOMAN'S WORLD   **Rs. 24**

J-403 CONVERSATIONAL   **Rs. 15**
       HINDI

J-408 HINDUSTANI FOR   **Rs. 15**
       THE TOURIST

J-442 HANDBOOK OF BABY   **Rs. 55**
       & CHILD CARE

J-459 HELP: FIRST AID FOR   **Rs. 35**
       EVERYDAY EMERGENCIES

J-461 UNDERSTANDING   **TOP**
       ELECTRONICS

J-499 ARABIC FOR   **Rs. 35**
       EVERYDAY USE

J-537 HANDBOOK OF   **Rs. 40**
       ENGLISH USAGE FOR
       EDITORS, WRITERS. . . .

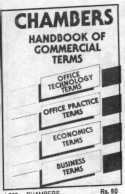

J-562 CHAMBERS HANDBOOK OF COMMERCIAL TERMS Rs. 60

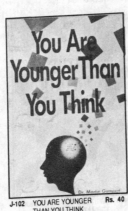

J-102 YOU ARE YOUNGER THAN YOU THINK Rs. 40

J-179 HINTS FOR SELF-CULTURE Rs. 40

J-192 1001 WAYS TO IMPROVE YOUR CONVERSATION & SPEECHES Rs. 45

J-463 REMEMBERING MADE EASY. Rs. 25

J-472 RAPID READING Rs. 36

J-536 ANGER: HOW   Rs. 70
TO LIVE WITH & WITHOUT IT

J-614 THE ART OF   Rs. 40
RELAXATION

J-655 HOW TO BE SELF-   Rs. 20
CONFIDENT

J-672 DYNAMICS OF MIND   Rs. 60
MANAGEMENT

JH-64 ATTITUDE   Rs.450
FORMATION & CHANGE

J-199 SPEAKER'S   Rs. 48
ENCYCLOPAEDIA OF
HUMOUR

J-224 SPEAKER'S HAND   Rs. 45
BOOK OF HUMOUR

J-235 LOVE IS A MAN'S AFFAIR — Rs. 4

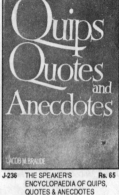

J-236 THE SPEAKER'S ENCYCLOPAEDIA OF QUIPS, QUOTES & ANECDOTES — Rs. 65

J-275 EXECUTIVE'S TREASURY OF HUMOUR FOR EVERY OCCASION — Rs. 50

J-335 BRAUDE'S TREASURY OF WIT & HUMOUR — Rs. 50

J-371 NEW TREASURY OF STORIES, SPEAKING & WRITING FOR EVERY OCCASION — Rs. 65

J-383 THE BEST JOKES OF ALL TIME & HOW TO TELL THEM — Rs. 50

J-468 SEX CAPADES — Rs. 10

J-469 SEXCLUSIVE — Rs. 10

J-470 SUPER SEX — Rs. 10

J-471 DO I HAVE A GIRL Rs. 15
FOR YOU

J-474 HANDBOOK OF Rs. 45
HUMOUR FOR SPEAKERS

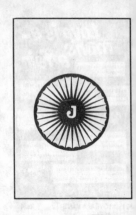

J-186 THE ART OF LOVE Rs. 45
MAKING

J-191 KAMASUTRA OF Rs. 45
VATSYAYANA
(ILLUSTRATED)

J-202 SEX IN MARRIAGE Rs. 45

J-365 SECRETS OF SEX Rs. 40

J-377 SENSOUS MAN Rs. 40

J-378   SENSOUS WOMAN   Rs. 40

J-423   TANTRA: THE SECRET   Rs. 35
POWER OF SEX

J-431   YOUR GUIDE TO LOVE   Rs. 35
& SEX.

J-435   SEX PROBLEMS &   Rs. 8
THEIR MANAGEMENT

J-465   EXPERT LOVEMAKING   Rs. 35

J-485   TANTRA : THE KEY   Rs. 45
TO SEXUAL POWER &
PLEASURE

J-489   THE SOCIAL POWER   Rs. 35
OF SEX

J-540   HOW TO MANAGE   TOP
YOUR HUSBAND

J-558   MASTERS & JOHNSON   Rs. 125
ON SEX & HUMAN LOVING

J-693 HOW TO WRITE LOVE   Rs. 75
LETTERS & LOVE POEMS

COOKERY

E. P. VEERASWAMY

INDIAN COOKERY

J-62   INDIAN COOKERY   Rs. 35

INDIAN COOKING

SAVITRI CHOWDHARY

J-187   INDIAN COOKING   Rs. 40

CURRIES OF INDIA

Harvey Day

J-189   CURRIES OF INDIA   Rs. 35

The Art of Vegetarian Cookery

BETTY WASON

J-268   THE ART OF VEGETA-   Rs. 36
RIAN COOKERY

GOOD FOOD FROM INDIA

SHANTI RANGARAO

J-300   GOOD FOOD FROM   Rs. 45
INDIA.

INDIAN COOKERY

S. MALHAN

J-342 INDIAN COOKERY Rs. 35

REGIONAL INDIAN RECIPES

RACHEL MUTHACHEN

J-343 REGIONAL INDIAN RECIPES Rs. 40

SIMPLIFIED INDIAN COOKERY

REBECCA JOSEPH

J-344 SIMPLIFIED INDIAN COOKERY Rs. 35

ADVENTURES IN INDIAN COOKING

MARY ATWOOD

J-382 ADVENTURES IN INDIAN COOKING Rs. 50

HOUSEWIFE'S GUIDE TO CHINESE COOKING

AROONA REEJHSINGHANI

J-392 HOUSEWIFE'S GUIDE TO CHINESE COOKING Rs. 35

THE ART OF SOUTH INDIAN COOKING

AROONA REEJHSINGHANI

J-404 ART OF SOUTH INDIAN COOKING Rs. 35

AROONA REEJHSINGHANI

Delights from Maharashtra

J-419 DELIGHTS FROM MAHARASHTRA Rs. 35

Delicious Bengali Dishes
AROONA REEJHSINGHANI

J-422 DELICIOUS BENGALI DISHES Rs. 35

Vegetarian Wonders From GUJARAT

AROONA REEJHSINGHANI

J-424 VEGETARIAN WONDERS FROM GUJARAT Rs. 35

J-445 COOKING THE PUNJABI WAY   Rs. 35

J-451 PARTY RECIPES   Rs. 35

J-496 TEMPTINGLY YOURS   Rs. 35

J-497 101 RECIPES   Rs. 35

J-501 DELICIOUSLY YOURS   Rs. 35

J-516 APPETISINGLY YOURS   Rs. 35

J-542 DELIGHTS FROM GOA   Rs. 35

J-552 OIL-LESS COOKING   Rs. 35

J-560 SOUTH INDIAN TIFFIN   Rs. 40

FOR RECIEVING
REGULAR INFORMATION
ON BOOKS, CONTACT
OR WRITE TO US
WITH COMPLETE ADDRESS.

J-596   MEXICAN COOKING   Rs. 35

HEALTH,
YOGA
& MEDICINE

J-296   YOGA : THE   Rs. 25
TECHNIQUE OF HEALTH
& HAPPINESS

J-308   YOGA FOR YOU   Rs. 35

J-309   FOREVER YOUNG   Rs. 30
FOREVER HEALTHY

J-349   YOGA FOR PHYSICAL   Rs. 45
FITNESS

J-351   YOGA : THE KEY TO LIFE Rs. 45

J-397 YOGA : MEANING, VALUES & PRACTICE Rs. 30

J-414 YOGA: ILLUSTRATED DICTIONARY Rs. 45

J-446 ALL ABOUT CONTACT LENSES Rs. 18

J-476 YOUR BODY IN HEALTH & SICKNESS Rs. 30

J-486 YOGA FOR HEALING Rs. 30

J-498 ALL ABOUT CATARACTS Rs. 25

J-500 EYE CARE Rs. 25

J-508 YOGA & YOUR HEART Rs. 50

J-517 CONQUERING CONSTIPATION Rs. 30

J-518   DEFEATING   Rs. 30
        DEPRESSION

J-549   DIET CURE FOR   Rs. 50
        COMMON AILMENTS

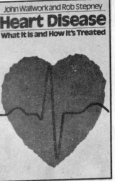

J-554   HEART DISEASE-   Rs. 50
        WHAT IT IS & HOW
        IT'S TREATED

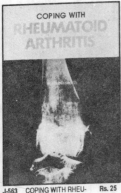

J-563   COPING WITH RHEU-   Rs. 25
        MATOID ARTHRITIS

J-564   COPING WITH   Rs. 25
        HEADACHES

J-607   YOUR NERVES: HOW   Rs. 20
        TO REDUCE TENSION

J-608   HOW TO OVERCOME   Rs. 20
        ANXIETY

J-610   HANDBOOK OF   Rs. 75
        MEDICINES FOR
        LAYMAN

J-618   A COMPLETE HAND-   Rs. 100
        BOOK OF NATURE CURE.

J-658   HATHA YOGA - THE   Rs. 150
        HIDDEN LANGUAGE

BRITISH MEDICAL ASSOCIATION FAMILY SERIES

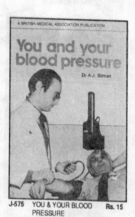

J-575   YOU & YOUR BLOOD   Rs. 15
        PRESSURE

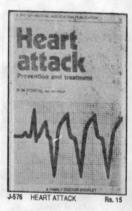

J-576   HEART ATTACK   Rs. 15

J-577   ARTHRITIS & JOINT   Rs. 15
        REPLACEMENT

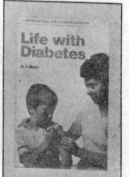

J-578   LIFE WITH DIABETES   Rs. 15

J-579   LIFE WITH ASTHAMA   Rs. 15

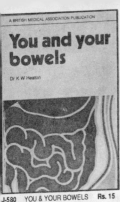

J-580　YOU & YOUR BOWELS　Rs. 15

J-581　KNOWING ABOUT SEX　Rs. 15

J-582　COPING WITH STRESS　Rs. 15

J-583　THE FACTS ABOUT DRUGS　Rs. 15

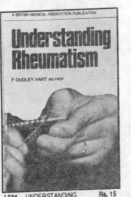

J-594　UNDERSTANDING RHEUMATISM　Rs. 15

J-521　LOOKING AFTER YOUR FEET　Rs. 15

J-622　YOUR NEW BABY　Rs. 15

J-623　AIDS　Rs. 15

J-624　HYSTERECTOMY　Rs. 15

J-625 LOOKING AFTER YOUR BACK — Rs. 15

J-626 TODDLERS COMMON PROBLEMS — Rs. 15

J-627 INCONTINENCE — Rs. 15

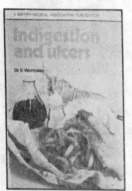

J-628 INDIGESTION & ULCERS — Rs. 15

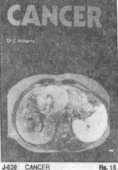

J-629 CANCER — Rs. 15

J-630 FEARS & PHOBIAS — Rs. 15

J-663 SNORING: CAUSES & PREVENTIVE MEASURES — Rs. 15

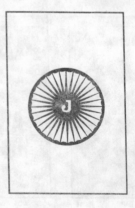

SPORTS
&
GAMES

J-272 FOREST OF THE Rs..25
NIGHT

J-273 SHIKAR Rs. 25

...3 HINTS ON TIGER Rs. 25
SHOOTING

J-326 JUNGLE LORE Rs. 25

J-379 TALES OF SHIKAR TOP

...2 BRAIN TEASERS Rs. 50

J-457 MAGIC FOR Rs. 35
BEGINNERS

J-458 CARD TRICKS FOR Rs. 35
BEGINNERS

J-487 KING OF KINGS: Rs. 25
THE STORY OF SIR
GARFIELD SOBERS

J-504 ALF GOVER'S CRICKET   Rs. 35
MANUAL

J-507 CRICKET'S   Rs. 20
UNFORGETTABLE
CLIFF-HANGERS

J-592 CHESS : A BEGINNER'S   Rs. 55
GUIDE

J-632 MIND TEASERS &   Rs 45
MIND PUZZLERS

J-676 THE WORLD'S BIGGEST   Rs. 70
RIDDLE BOOK IN
THE WORLD

J-692 THE WORLD'S BEST   Rs. 50
PARTY GAMES

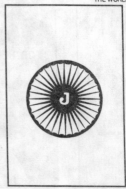

COMPUTERS

J-555 UNDERSTANDING FORTRAN — Rs. 110

J-565 PROGRAMMING IN BASIC — Rs. 100

J-566 THE SPIRIT OF C — Rs. 120

J-589 A FIRST BOOK OF C — Rs. 95

J-590 WORKING WITH LOTUS 1-2-3 — Rs. 100

J-591 UNDERSTANDING & USING dBASE III PULS — Rs. 60

J-593 PROGRAMMING & PROBLEM SOLVING WITH PASCAL — Rs. 90

J-594 UNDERSTANDING & USING WORDSTAR 4.0 — Rs. 65

J-601 REALTIME SOFTWARE **Rs. 60**
FOR SMALL SYSTEMS

J-612 UNDERSTANDING & **Rs. 125**
USING dBASE IV

J-613 UNDERSTANDING **Rs. 90**
PASCAL TURBO VERSION

J-631 UNDERSTANDING & **Rs. 90**
USING LOTUS 1-2-3

J-635 ILLUSTRATED **Rs. 80**
WORDSTAR PROFESS-
IONAL RELEASE 5.0

J-636 ILLUSTRATED QUICK **Rs. 90**
BASIC 4.0

J-638 FORTRAN 77 **Rs. 112**

J-680 ILLUSTRATED Q **Rs. 125**
BASIC FOR MSDOS 5.0

J-682 ILLUSTRATED **Rs. 115**
PAGE MAKER 4.0

J-684   A QUICK COURSE IN   **Rs. 75**
WORD FOR WINDOWS

J-685   A QUICK COURSE IN   **Rs. 75**
LOTUS 1-2-3

J-686   A QUICK COURSE IN   **Rs. 75**
DOS

J-687   A QUICK COURSE   **Rs. 75**
IN WINDOWS 3.1

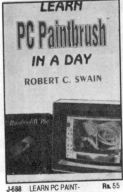

J-688   LEARN PC PAINT-   **Rs. 55**
BRUSH IN A DAY

J-689   A QUICK COURSE IN   **Rs. 75**
EXCEL-4

J-690   LEARN PAL IN A DAY   **Rs. 85**

J-691   LEARN PARADOX IN   **Rs. 65**
A DAY

J-701   GRAPHIC DESIGN AND
VISUALISATION

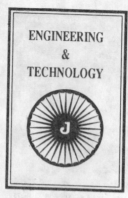

ENGINEERING & TECHNOLOGY

J-683 LABORATORY MANUAL **Rs. 35**
IN ENVIRONMENTAL
ENGINEERING

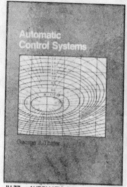

JH-77 AUTOMATIC CON- **Rs. 350(HB)**
J-659 TROL SYSTEMS **Rs.95 (PB)**

JH-88 MACHINE COMPO- **Rs. 750**
NENT DESIGN (2 VOLS.)

JH-97 ELECTRONIC CIRCUIT **Rs. 650**
ANALYSIS & DESIGN

JH-98 PRINCIPLES OF **Rs. 975**
COMMUNICATIONS

JH-99 HYDRAULIC **Rs. 900**
ENGINEERING

JH-102 THE COMPLETE **Rs. 495**
COMMUNICATIONS
HANDBOOK

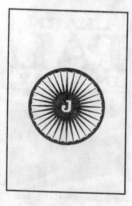

SPECIAL SUBJECTS

JH-15 MASS COMMUNICATION IN INDIA (Under Revision) TOP

JH-74 A PRACTICAL MANUAL OF COLON CLASSIFICATION Rs. 290

JH-89 LIBRARY USER STUDIES Rs. 390

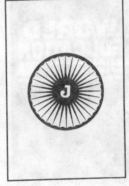

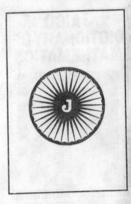

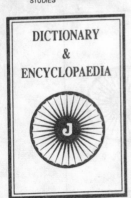

DICTIONARY & ENCYCLOPAEDIA

JH-73 MIZORAM ENCYCLOPAEDIA Rs. 875

JH-81 JAICO ILLUSTRATED ENCYCLOPAEDIA OF TECHNICAL TERMS (2 Vols.) Rs. 750(HB)
JH-671 Rs. 95(PB)

JAICO DICTIONARY OF COMPUTERS

JH-82 JAICO DICTIONARY Rs. 450
J-668 OF COMPUTERS Rs. 75 (PB)

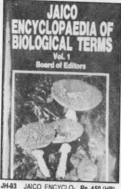

JAICO ENCYCLOPAEDIA OF BIOLOGICAL TERMS
Vol. 1
Board of Editors

JH-83 JAICO ENCYCLO- Rs. 450 (HB)
J-670 PAEDIA OF BIOLOGICAL Rs. 95 (PB)
TERMS (2 Vols.)

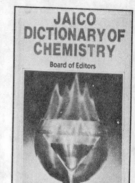

JAICO DICTIONARY OF CHEMISTRY
Board of Editors

JH-84 JAICO DICTIONARY Rs. 450(HB)
J669 OF CHEMISTRY Rs. 75 (PB)

JAICO DICTIONARY OF MATHEMATICS
Board of Editors

JH-85 JAICO DICTIONARY Rs. 450 (HB)
J-671 OF MATHEMATICS. Rs. 75 (PB)

WORLD EDUCATION ENCYCLOPAEDIA
Price Rs. 3500.00 (3 Vol. Set)

JH-94 WORLD EDUCATION Rs. 3500
ENCLYCLOPEDIA (Per Set)
(3 Vols.)

JAICO DICTIONARY OF TELE-COMMUNICATIONS
JOHN GRAHAM
REVISED AND UPDATED BY SUE J. LOWE

JH-96 JAICO DICTIONARY Rs. 450
OF TELECOMMUNICATIONS

POLITICAL ENCYCLOPAEDIA
CHRIS COOK

JH-101 WORLD POLITICAL Rs. 775
ENCYCLOPAEDIA

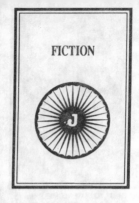

FICTION

J

THE BEST OF
EDGAR WALLACE

J-597   THE BEST OF   Rs. 95
         EDGAR WALLACE

THE MAMMOTH BOOK OF
MURDER
Richard Glyn Jones

J-641   MAMMOTH BOOK   Rs. 100
         OF MURDER STORIES

THE MAMMOTH BOOK OF
PRIVATE EYE
STORIES
Edited by Bill Pronzini and Martin H. Greenberg

J-646   THE MAMMOTH BOOK   Rs. 100
         OF PRIVATE EYE STORIES

THE MAMMOTH BOOK OF
SHORT
HORROR
NOVELS
Edited by Mike Ashley

COMPLETE AND UNABRIDGED

10 short novels by
Stephen King
Lucius Shepard
Russell Kirk
T.E.D. Klein
David Case
John Metcalfe
Oliver Onions
A.C. Benson
Arthur Conan Doyle
Algernon Blackwood

J-647   MAMMOTH BOOK   Rs. 100
         OF SHORT HORROR NOVELS

THE MAMMOTH BOOK OF
GOLDEN AGE
SCIENCE FICTION

Presented by Isaac Asimov
Complete and unabridged

J-648   THE MAMMOTH   Rs. 125
         BOOK OF GOLDEN AGE
         SCIENCE FICTION

THE MAMMOTH BOOK OF
CLASSIC
SCIENCE
FICTION

Presented by Isaac Asimov
Complete and unabridged

J-649   THE MAMMOTH BOOK   Rs. 130
         OF CLASSIC SCIENCE FICTION

THE MAMMOTH BOOK OF
SPY
THRILLERS
3

J-650   THE MAMMOTH BOOK   Rs. 100
         OF SPY THRILLERS

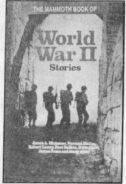

THE MAMMOTH BOOK OF
World
War II
Stories

James A. Michener, Norman Mailer,
Robert Leckey, Paul Gallico, Irwin Shaw,
James Jones and many others

J-651   THE MAMMOTH BOOK   Rs. 100
         OF WORLD WAR II STORIES

J-654   THE MAMMOTH BOOK   Rs. 100
OF GREAT DETECTIVE
STORIES

JH-92   THE WORLD IN MY   Rs. 75
POCKET & THE PAIN IN THE
BOTTLE JAMES HADLEY CHASE

JH-93   YOU HAVE YOURSELF   Rs. 75
A DEAL; TELL IT TO THE BIRDS-
JAMES HADLEY CHASE

MISCELLANEOUS

J-553   JAICO BOOK OF BABY   Rs 20
NAMES WITH MEAN-   Rs.120
INGS & EXPLANATIONS (Boxed)

THE TIGER OF
RAJASTHAN
COLONEL KESRI SINGH

J-270   THE TIGER OF   Rs. 25
RAJASTHAN

J-633   INTERPRET YOUR   Rs. 20
DREAMS

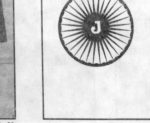

PALMISTRY, ASTROLOGY, GRAPHOLOGY

THE DICTIONARY OF PALMISTRY
J.S. BRIGHT

J-128   THE DICTIONARY OF   Rs. 30
        PALMISTRY

PALMISTRY MADE EASY
J. S. Bright

J-232   PALMISTRY MADE   Rs. 30
        EASY

Astrology

How to cast your own horoscope

SHRIDHAR B. DHAMANKAR
M.P. LAGU

J-503   ASTROLOGY   Rs. 25

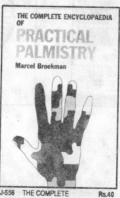

THE COMPLETE ENCYCLOPAEDIA OF
PRACTICAL PALMISTRY
Marcel Broekman

J-556   THE COMPLETE   Rs.40
        ENCYCLOPAEDIA OF
        PALMISTRY

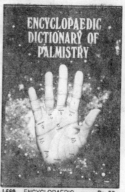

ENCYCLOPAEDIC DICTIONARY OF PALMISTRY

J-569   ENCYCLOPAEDIC   Rs. 55
        DICTIONARY OF PALMISTRY

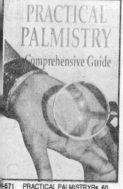

PRACTICAL PALMISTRY
Comprehensive Guide

J-571   PRACTICAL PALMISTRY Rs. 60
        A COMPREHENSIVE GUIDE

MIRACLES OF NUMEROLOGY

J-619   MIRACLE OF   Rs. 55
        NUMEROLOGY

BEJAN DARUWALLA'S BOOK OF
STAR SIGNS
NUMEROLOGY 1
CHINESE
ASTROLOGY

ALSO INCLUDES
ANNUAL FORECASTS OF
ALL STARS FOR 1991 & 1992
WORLD HOROSCOPE IN THE 90's

J-637   BEJAN DARUWALLA'S   Rs. 60
        BOOK OF STAR
        SIGNS, NUMEROLOGY,
        CHINESE ASTROLOGY.

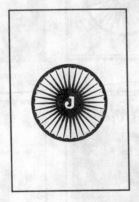

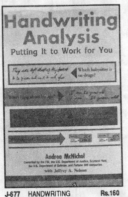

Andrea McNichol
with Jeffrey A. Nelson

J-677   HANDWRITING   Rs.160
             ANALYSIS